Not For Ourselves Alone

Not For Ourselves Alone

*The Legacies of Two Pioneers
of Black Higher Education
in the United States*

Hakim J. Lucas

Virginia Union University

INFORMATION AGE PUBLISHING, INC.
Charlotte, NC • www.infoagepub.com

Library of Congress Cataloging-in-Publication Data

A CIP record for this book is available from the Library of Congress
http://www.loc.gov

ISBN: 978-1-64113-788-1 (Paperback)
      978-1-64113-789-8 (Hardcover)
      978-1-64113-790-4 (ebook)

Printed in the United States of America

I dedicate this work to my beloved family and dear friends.
I dedicate it to all the people who have consistently labored in the support
of all my endeavors and have encouraged and shown true agape along the way.
It is equally dedicated to all the readers who will find me in this work and all the
young men and women at Virginia Union University and sister HBCUs
that will find themselves in this work.

Contents

Preface

This project is the outcome of my academic musings, since my undergraduate years at Morehouse College. Having been raised by two ministers and educators, my earliest recollections include Black church practices and educational reinforcements from my parents. My formative years at Morehouse College were the intellectual platform, which granted me the theoretical means to frame the questions this project sets out to address. "What makes Black higher education important?"; "What is its historical trajectory in the larger context of American history?"; "What visions were the incentives for its rise?"; and lastly, "How do we bridge its rich and distinctive history with the current demands of Black higher education in the 21st century?" These are the pressing questions which coalesced and drove my academic pursuits from Morehouse College to the completion of my doctoral studies at Fordham University.

The pragmatic dimension of the project was furnished by first-hand experiences from my leadership roles in Black church communities and Black college academic settings. My earliest observations of organizational dynamics through roles in the pulpit and administration granted hands-on experience of the continuity between the Black church's tradition and Black institutions of higher education. As I compose this preface, I acknowledge the level of influence that these questions and the goal to improve the shortcomings that I observed, exert upon my current role as president of Virginia Union University. As such, this project is intended for anyone who wishes to grasp the genealogy of Black higher education in the United States. Also, it

Not For Ourselves Alone, pages xi–xii
Copyright © 2019 by Information Age Publishing

is my humble hope that this project will inspire other presidents and administrators of Black higher educational institutions to chronicle their journeys in light of the historic missions of both Black institutions. Ultimately, as it will become apparent throughout the project the shared vision is to design the most suitable strategies to train future leaders to meet the sociocultural, political, and economic demands of the present and future.

I believe the importance of this work is found in its attempt to chart a new course in how we think about the need to reconcile the vision and foundation of Black higher education within the context of global educational expectations. The book explores the roots of Black higher education, theory of education and community leadership, historic concepts, theories, and ideals used to educate African-Americans. Also, it provides a historical account of Black higher education during Emancipation, Reconstruction, and Jim Crow; using the historical accounts of Rev. Dr. Payne and Rev. Dr. Joseph missions to build Wilberforce University and Morehouse College to inform how educational leaders can provide leadership in the 21st century.

This research makes it plain that the establishment of Black higher education in the United States was born out of the similar vision held by these two leaders and their unwavering commitment to serve Black communities. I have learned from the historical accounts of Rev. Dr. Payne and Rev. Dr. Joseph that *servant leadership* is the suitable model to guide the presidency of higher institutions, as it compels the vision of a president to be in tune with the social, economic, and cultural expressions of students, while developing curriculum that trains them to innovate their present context in view of the future.

My hope is this book secures its place in the literature in virtue of the fact that there is no specific literature about founding presidents of Black higher education and the questions it sets out to answer. I attempt to provide a thorough account of Black higher education among African-American communities during each challenging period of the 20th century and how each antecedent set of challenges shapes its future. I pray this book will be useful to educators and laypeople who are earnest in their search for the roots of Black higher education, what makes historically Black colleges and universities still relevant in the 21st century, serving as a handbook for leaders, administrators, and faculty of higher educational institutions. For over 200 years, Black colleges and universities have been at the center of the African-American community. It is our hope this book signifies 200 more to come, as their legacy is not for ourselves alone.

Acknowledgments

I would like to acknowledge and thank the library and special reserves staff at the Wilberforce University and Morehouse College for their time and assistance towards the completion of this study.

Special thanks to Dr. Bruce Cooper, Dr. Gerald Cattaro, Rev. Dr. Edison O. Jackson, Rev. Dr. Barbara Austin Lucas, and Dr. Anthony B. Pinn for the years of guidance, support and encouragement and hours spent mentoring, advising, and editing this work.

Finally, I acknowledge and thank God, the Most Blessed One, for allowing me the opportunity to be God's scribe.

1

Historical Questions

Overview of Study

For over 200 years Black colleges and universities have been at the intellectual center of the African-American community. The legacy of these institutions has been to equip African Americans with the skills, tools, and competencies needed to be successful professional, educated, and cultured human beings. Given its rich history, Black higher education in the United States provides a most interesting subject for a comparative research study. In order to delineate the central role of Black higher education, the following study will focus on Wilberforce University and Morehouse College as two institutions with a long legacy in gearing African Americans with the skills, tools, and competencies needed to be successful professional, educated, and cultured human beings.

Founding Leadership

Wilberforce University was founded in Wilberforce, Ohio by European Methodist ministers in 1856. However, it was closed during the Civil War due to the lack of financial support in the Northern Midwest for the

Not For Ourselves Alone, pages 1–16
Copyright © 2019 by Information Age Publishing

education of Black people. In 1865, Bishop Daniel Alexander Payne led the African Methodist Episcopal Church's purchase of the university and merged it with the previously established Union College founded in 1843. Having been a founding member of the board of directors when the school temporarily closed between 1863–1865, Bishop Payne assumed the leadership of Wilberforce University as its first president between 1865 and 1876.

The second institution, Morehouse College, was founded in 1867 by a group of Baptist preachers from Augusta, Georgia. Their mission was to train young Black men to enter the Christian ministry, under the auspices of what was then known as the Augusta Baptist Seminary. Morehouse College was founded as a single-sex institution aimed at the education of African-American males. Morehouse College is historically significant because it is the first major college founded in the confederate South post-Civil War, while adhering to its mission (Goldman & Buyers, 2005, p. 343). Rev. Dr. Joseph Robert, a white Baptist minister, served as its first president. His tenure provides an interesting opportunity to assess the challenges of European American leadership in a minority serving institution, particularly in the old confederate South during a most trying time in U.S. history.

Research Questions

By relying on the educational models of Wilberforce University and Morehouse College, this study gathered historical artifacts that provide critical responses to the following research questions:

> What were the similarities and differences between the social, historical, political, and cultural forces that led to the founding of the colleges? What were the similar and different motivations and interests of the founding leaders? What were the similar and different effects of these founding leaders on their institutions in their time period? What similar and different supports did these institutions receive from their religious organizations? What can we learn from the impact of these institutions on Black higher education over the last 150 years?

Narrative Overview

The author of this project sets out to answer the aforementioned research questions through the following seven chapters:

Chapter 1, "Historical Questions," provides an overview of the research topic and contextualizes the study by identifying the research questions. This chapter provides a brief introduction to the history of Black higher education during Reconstruction in the United States. It then describes the institutional context of the time period to show the need for research on this topic and to articulate the study's significance.

Chapter 2, "Historical Methodology," outlines the historical method and approach to this study. This chapter defines and explains the selection of scientific management as the educational theory underpinning this study. It also defines and explains the use of Dr. Jim Laub's renowned servant leadership, *organizational leadership assessment* (OLA) model. This chapter also details the historical research methodologies used to establish protocols for data collection, processing, and interpretation. The discussion of methodology defines the approach to textual criticism, which is used for analysis of primary source materials (letters, journals, newspapers, and autobiographies, these stories chronicle the efforts of slaves and freedmen to access their human rights).

Chapter 3, "Historical Context," articulates the central problem, critical issues, and historical context that have inspired this research study. This chapter assesses the social, historical, political, and cultural forces that led to the founding of the colleges by providing a historiography of Black education during Reconstruction, while detailing its development and continued struggles. This chapter also develops the thesis that Black education during Reconstruction was the natural by-product of the pre-existing struggle of African-American communities to achieve empowerment and self-improvement.

Chapter 4, "Founding Presidents and Their Colleges," provides a biographical introduction to the personal and professional experiences of Bishop Daniel Alexander Payne during his tenure as president of Wilberforce University, 1865–1876 and Rev. Dr. Joseph Robert's tenure as president of Morehouse College, 1871–1884. Accordingly, the focus of this chapter is fourfold. First, it elaborates the core aspects of Dr. Daniel Alexander Payne's tenure as president of Wilberforce University. It, then, shifts to draw out the phases of the historical development of Wilberforce University. Thirdly, it elaborates the key constituents of Dr. Joseph Robert's presidency of Morehouse College. And lastly, it maps out the historical development of Morehouse College: (a) President Payne, (b) the historical developments of Wilberforce, (c) President Robert, and (d) the historical developments of Morehouse. Moreover, utilizing the historical methodologies discussed in Chapter 3, this chapter will assess these founding presidents' motivations, interests, and the professional accomplishments and challenges of these founding presidents. It concludes with some reflections about how institutional support affected their individual legacy in the context of the time period. It then draws conclusions about how the types of supports each received from their respective institutions affected their presidential legacy in the time period.

Chapter 5, "Institutional Comparisons, 1865–1884," focuses on conducting institutional and leadership profile assessments (this statement is ambiguous and needs to be rephrased. Do you mean how institutional and leadership profile assessments are conducted? Or how institutional and leadership profile assessments should be conducted?). The institutional assessment includes a demographical and mission-based comparison of the colleges. The leadership assessment compares and contrasts each president's impact and influence on their respective institutions, and the similarities and differences of their presidential leadership.

Chapter 6, "Implications and Meanings for Higher Education," the conclusion builds from the research questions to determine what can be learned from the impact of these institutions on Black higher education over the last 150 years. And how their accomplishments can be used as guidelines for contemporary institutional development, curricula development, Christian education, gender studies, the improvement of Black colleges, and lastly how to mold exemplary presidents to lead these unique institutions.

Historical Context

Reconstruction

Reconstruction was a period in which political, social, and economic ideologies were debated as a means to influence the restoration and revitalization of the republic, particularly in the Southern states. These ideologies were media to conceive the ideal America as a cohesive republic. Ronald E. Butchart (1980) summarizes:

> The context for a reconstructed South was established by emancipation and Northern victory; the content, however, was forged in the fires of conflict between the goals and aspirations of Northern whites, blacks, planters, and poor whites, mediated by the power held by, and the alliances formed between, northern and southern elites. (p. xi)

Moreover, Reconstruction stands as a defining turning point in the evolution of a nation engaged in a process of re-envisioning the ideals espoused by its founding fathers in the U.S. Constitution. This process left lasting effects on the country's political, social, and economic practices post-Civil War and post-emancipation. Fitzgerald (2007) identifies the political climate of 19th century United States as the most dominant force, which determines: the success or failure of Reconstruction. He clarifies the historical significance of Reconstruction, explaining it as a process of negotiating the reunification of the states, at the heart of which was the easement of the Southern, democrat, plantation owning, middle-class, and Christian's political, social, and economic concerns about states' rights and black labor (Fitzgerald, 2007, p. x).

Reconstruction and reconstriction are key words that adequately represent the constant struggles of national leaders to chart a course through the often stormy political climate of 19th century United States. By the summer of 1877, the national sentiments towards racial justice, as a cornerstone of Reconstruction, had diluted and the common view brought to the fore the challenges of ensuring state protection of civil rights, especially, if it necessitated military action and federal support. Governor Chamberlain of South Carolina, after hearing the outcome of the presidential election of 1876, departed the capital with the following words:

> Today—April 10, 1877—by the order of the President whom your [freedmen] votes alone rescued from overwhelming defeat, the Government of the United States abandons you . . . with the full knowledge that the lawful Government of the state will be speedily overthrown. (Fitzgerald, 2007, p. 206)

President Hayes's desire to form a new political base to include Southern democrats made it easier to substitute a political ideology of racial justice for one of racial tolerance, a more acceptable outcome of Reconstruction. This atmosphere of racial tolerance set the stage for Black colleges, which emerged in this historical context. This study investigates various primary source materials and other historical accounts of the time period to provide a suitable account of the social, historical, political, and cultural forces that led to the founding of these colleges.

The Roots of Black Higher Education

The study of Black higher education develops from post-emancipation to the civil rights eras of U.S. history, c1864 to c1965 (see Table 1.1). This historical time period can be characterized as an educational golden age for African Americans in which their commitment to education was often challenged by social and political indifference and lack of resources. Harriet Beecher Stowe (1879) summarizes this time period best in observing that "newly freed Blacks at word of their emancipation rushed not to grogshops but to schoolrooms, acknowledging the importance of spelling books as bread and teachers as a necessity of life" (Anderson, 1988, p. 5). The

TABLE 1.1 Transformative Outcomes of the Civil Rights Movement

African-American Civil Rights Event	Negative Experience Prior to or After Event	Transformational Strategy	Transformative Outcome
Slave Insurrections (17th and 18th Century): Through the 17th and 18th century, as slavery and the importation of slaves proliferated various resistance occurred.	Insurrections most certainly led to martyrdom (which could be considered as a positive event); however, Europeans developed brutal ways to prevent insurrection (e.g., branding, lynching, castration, separation of family to instill fear).	Violent Protests: – 1739, 20 slaves in SC – 1800, Gabriel Prosser – 1811, 500 slaves in LA – 1822, Denmark Vessey – 1831, Gabriel Prosser – 1859, John Brown	Was the root of African American civil protest in the United States, and began the process of creating a culture of survival.
The Movement Back to Africa: Proposal led by Thomas Jefferson	Treated the African Americans as commodities that could be imported and exported.	Federal funds were dedicated to the newly established American Colonization Society in 1816.	The colony of Liberia in West Africa was founded on January 7, 1822 when 20,000 freed slaves were sent back to Africa.
The Missouri Compromise (1819): Talmadge's Amendment to Missouri's request for statehood.	The Missouri compromise set in motion a debate over the spread of slavery throughout the states, and the balance of power needed between southern and northern states.	Missouri was admitted as a slave state, and Maine was admitted as a free state.	The federal government began to have more impact in the activities of the states.
Fugitive Slave Act of 1848 and Compromise of 1850: Made it illegal to transport or harbor slaves across state lines and admitted lands won from the Mexican war.	The issue of slavery continued to stir animosity between the northern and southern states. Bounty Hunters also became a business opportunity.	The Fugitive Slave Laws stifled the abolitionist movement as it became a felony to transport slaves along state lines. Through the Compromise of 1850, Henry Clay proposed that New Mexico and Utah be admitted as slave states and California be admitted as a free state.	

(continued)

TABLE 1.1 Transformative Outcomes of the Civil Rights Movement (continued)

African-American Civil Rights Event	Negative Experience Prior to or After Event	Transformational Strategy	Transformative Outcome
Civil War (1861): First shots rang out at Fort Sumter as the Confederacy of Southern States declared their independence.	Began the fight between the north and the south over state sovereignty, and the unbreakable union.	Violent protest erupts.	The Northern states won and from hence, the United States was an unbreakable Union, with a representative federalist government.
Emancipation Proclamation (1863): Given by President Abraham Lincoln, abolished slavery in the United States.	African Americans were slaves, and freedom was a privilege.	Executive order	African Americans' freedom was considered as rights for citizens and human beings.
13th Amendment: Post Civil War was an official amendment to the Constitution of the United States.	Involuntary servitude is abolished and sharecropping became a legal form of slavery.	Congressional Amendment	Emergence of debate regarding the meaning of freedom.
15th Amendment: Gave all citizens the right to vote.	African Americans were left out of the political process.	Congressional Amendment	More African Americans in U.S. History to date were elected to political office.
End of Reconstruction: The Hayes and Tilden compromise	The institution of the Grandfather Clause prevented Blacks from voting in the South and the KKK began to arise as a social inhibitor.		African Americans formed social groups and began to organize their own institutions (self-help).
Plessy vs. Ferguson (1896): The Supreme Court decision that ruled separate but equal was Constitutional.	African Americans are forced to live in segregated social environments.	The U.S. Supreme Court decided that separate but equal was constitutional, and resulted in the enactment of the Jim Crow laws in the South.	African Americans formed social organizations to fight for change through the legal system (NAACP).

(continued)

TABLE 1.1 Transformative Outcomes of the Civil Rights Movement (continued)

African-American Civil Rights Event	Negative Experience Prior to or After Event	Transformational Strategy	Transformative Outcome
Great Depression (1921–1935)	The Great Depression was a hard time for African Americans as their unemployment rate was over 50%.	African Americans began to support the Democratic Party, specifically, the programs of President Roosevelt.	President Roosevelt established the Black Cabinet, a collection of Black leaders to advise him on various issues and a Civil Rights Section in the Justice Department to monitor the treatment of Blacks in the United States.
WWII—Executive Order 8802 (1941): Black leaders fought for equal hiring practices lobbying the president to take action.	African Americans were denied freedoms of employment in federal or state jobs.	Lobbying presidents to enact bills to improve the social status of African Americans.	President Roosevelt issued the Executive order and African Americans began to arise as national leaders with prominence in relation to the White House.
Democratic Convention of 1948	The Dixiecrats assumed much control of the agenda of the Democratic Party.	The northern (liberal) states proposed an agenda to fight segregation and discrimination in employment and industries.	The Democrats became the party of choice for African Americans.
(1948): President Truman issued an Executive order mandating equal treatment and opportunity in the armed forces without regard to race, color, religion, or national origin.	African Americans are denied access to the armed forces and other governmental departments.	Lobbying of government officials and initiating court legislation process.	African American men gained access to the armed forces.

(continued)

TABLE 1.1 Transformative Outcomes of the Civil Rights Movement (continued)

African-American Civil Rights Event	Negative Experience Prior to or After Event	Transformational Strategy	Transformative Outcome
Brown vs. Board of Education of Topeka, Kansas (1954): U.S. Supreme Court ruled in the case of Brown vs. the Board of Education of Topeka, Kansas unanimously that separate schools were inherently unequal.	1. African Americans maintained segregated educational institutions from European Americans, particularly in resources. 2. European Americans in the south locked students out and violently protested the end to segregation (i.e., Daisy Bates and the Arkansas Nine)	In the case of Daisy Bates and the Little Rock nine, the Arkansas National Guard had to be called in to assure students' integration. The use of legislation by the NAACP was the tool of transformation.	Students were eventually allowed access to public education in White schools.
Rosa Parks (1955): Mrs. Rosa Parks in Montgomery, Alabama refused to give up her seat to a European American.	This civil disobedience ended in the arrest of Mrs. Parks and provoked a public outcry.	This singular event galvanized local civil rights leadership to begin protests that culminated into the Montgomery Bus Boycott. Leaders founded the Montgomery Improvement Association (MIA) and Dr. Martin Luther King Jr. was elected as its first leader.	In 1956 the U.S. Supreme Court decision banning segregated buses.
The Freedom Rides: Occurred in the Summer of 1961 when college students assumed responsibility of the struggle for civil rights.	African Americans had to ride segregated transportation systems. The Freedom Rides were risky endeavors given that many young African Americans were attacked and many African Americans lost their lives.	This movement was planned by college students, the Congress of Racial Equality (CORE) and Student Nonviolent Coordinating Committee (SNCC), which in the Summer of 1961 planned to desegregate interstate bus travel and waiting areas in bus terminals.	Students became the foundation and backbone of the African American push for civil rights. Interstate Commerce Commission banned segregation at bus terminals in November 1961.

(continued)

TABLE 1.1 Transformative Outcomes of the Civil Rights Movement (continued)

African-American Civil Rights Event	Negative Experience Prior to or After Event	Transformational Strategy	Transformative Outcome
The March on Washington (1963)	African Americans waited years for civil rights legislation to be passed, however, they failed to fulfill their expectations to no avail.	A. Phillip Randolph and other Black leaders decided to protest by staging a march (temporary takeover) on Washington to show the solidarity of the American public for civil rights of African American communities in 1963. 250,000 men, women, and children gathered to protest.	The March showed the strength of the civil rights movement when considered as a community outcry, and not sporadic, or independent movements.
1964 Civil Rights Act	No federal legislation strong enough to curve discrimination on the state levels.

The Civil Rights Act was a result of the assassination of President Kennedy, and countless other leaders. | The act included 11 titles that covered a variety of issues, called entitlements, specifically, prohibiting discrimination by private employers against any person because of race, color, sex, religion, or national origin. | African Americans could defend their freedoms in all courts empowered by the institution. Furthermore, no compliance was a federal offense. |
| *The EEOC and Affirmative Action* | Civil Rights legislation did not extend to the private sector. | Through an Executive order, President Johnson established what is called Title VII—The Equal Employment Opportunity Commission. | Title VII assures that all members of the private sector who hold contracts with the United States must abide by civil rights legislation. |

(continued)

TABLE 1.1 Transformative Outcomes of the Civil Rights Movement (continued)

African-American Civil Rights Event	Negative Experience Prior to or After Event	Transformational Strategy	Transformative Outcome
1965 Voting Rights Act	African Americans had to take literacy tests, or were prevented by local voting registrars from voting.	This Act of Congress allowed the Attorney General's Office to replace all County and Local registrars with Federal Registrars. All voting activities would be managed by the federal government.	From continued protest, all African Americans over the age of 21 were allowed the right to vote, under the protection of the Federal government.
1990 Civil Rights Act	African Americans feared that the gains they had made over the years were being eroded by claims of reverse racism.	African American leaders lobbied Congressional representatives.	Burden of proof for all discrimination cases were imposed upon the employer to prove they were not discriminating.

droves of African Americans seeking an education as the primary vehicle of self and communal empowerment resulted in exorbitant costs associated with the full socioeconomic integration of freed people into U.S. society that burdened the Bureau of Refugees, Freedmen, and Abandoned Lands. Thus, freedmen began to take a more aggressive approach to financing their own education, which is exemplified in Virginia where freedmen paid for 153 plots and schoolhouses by 1870 (Butchart, 1980, p. 11).

Documented in this time period are the works of many African-American leaders who published various tracts, articles, and books, while organizing their own schools to disseminate their beliefs in the importance of Black higher education. These works include: Charles C. Andrew's (1830) *History of the New York African Free Schools;* Frederick Douglass's autobiography (1840); the writings of Martin Delaney (1847) specifically in his publication the *North Star* (co-founded with Douglass); and Leonard Black's autobiography (1847). These publications represent a body of literature, which circulated among African-American communities of the South and North that stirred the desire for education, showing it as an essential part of their story of triumph. Through the use of nonfiction, African Americans were able to deduce how education played a critical role in motivating popular freedmen to risk death for freedom and overcome fear to champion the causes of the race. As such, these works were central in arousing interest in Black higher education.

This study examines the literature of this golden age of Black higher education, while being more attentive to the publications of the religious community that supported Wilberforce and Morehouse. It is undeniable that African-American and European churches played a major role in sponsoring and building schools for ex-slaves. Accordingly, a major goal of this research is to detail the extent of this support. One Freedmen's Bureau superintendent of education in Kentucky said in 1867: "The places of worship owned by the colored people are almost the only available school houses in the state" (Anderson, 1988, p. 13). Under the light of this fact, a review of the literature produced by these organizations is critical to understand the preliminary infrastructure of Black higher education at the time of the founding of Black colleges.

Institutional Context

The history of Black higher education in the United States cannot be considered apart from the context in which these educational institutions were established. Black higher education was built on the foundation of freedmen's self-reliance and deep-seated desire to create, control, and sustain schools for themselves and their children (Anderson, 1988, p. 5). To appreciate this aforementioned desire, one must consider the great obstacles that 18th and 19th century freedmen overcame to win the right to an education. Fueled by the opposition of slaveholders and southern planters to their literacy, education for Blacks in the South and North was a dangerous endeavor.

Historically, as literacy increased amongst slaves, so did the number of insurrections, protests, and escapes. Examples of these include rebellions led by Denmark Vesey, David Walker, John Brown, and Nat Turner (Bullock, 1967, p. 14). David Walker would write in his publication, *The Appeal*, in 1829:

> For although the destruction of the oppressors, God may not effect by the oppressed, yet the Lord our God will bring other destruction upon them, for not infrequently will he cause them to rise up against the others to be split, divided, and oppress each other, and sometimes to open hostilities with sword in hand. (Wright, 2009, p. 144)

Insurrections and rebellions of this nature were in most cases believed by Southern White planters to be the result of literacy. In efforts to suppress these early freedom movements, southern planters organized and lobbied state legislatures to prohibit education amongst slaves. The first state to legally prohibit the education of slaves was South Carolina. The Assembly's statute read:

> And whereas, the having of slaves taught to write, or suffering them to be employed in writing, may be attended with great inconveniences; be it therefore enacted...that all and every person and persons whatsoever, who shall hereafter teach, or cause any slave or slaves to be taught, to write, or shall use or employ any slave as a scribe in any manner of writing whatsoever, hereafter taught to write, every such person and persons, shall, for every such offence, forfeit the sum of one hundred pounds current money. (Wright, 2009, p. 371)

As with the South Carolina Assembly, other southern states would follow suit in implementing laws through state legislatures to restrict African-Americans' rights. Many Southern states called these guidelines and restrictions Black Codes (or Laws). Black Codes legally prohibited Blacks from voting, being members of juries, testifying against Whites, leasing or owning property, banned interracial marriage, and punished Blacks more severely than Whites for committing a crime (Murrin et al., 2008, p. 631).

In the case of South Carolina's Black Laws, the vagrancy statues, for example, went as far as allowing local police to arrest and fine virtually any Black man for being on the public streets without a specific purpose. If the fine could not be paid, he was forced to work on the farm, often the one owned and operated by his former master (Boydston, Cullather, Lewis, McGerr, & Oakes, 2004, p. 376). In the case of Mississippi, their 1865 Black Codes prohibited not only vagrancy, but also forbid landownership, alcohol or firearm possession, and interracial marriage. Of the latter, Section 3 of the civil rights law states:

> that it shall not be lawful for any freedman, free Negroes, or mulatto to intermarry with any white person; nor for any white person to intermarry with any freedman, free Negro, or mulatto shall be deemed guilty of a felony and, on conviction thereof, shall be confined in the state penitentiary for life. (Wright, 2009, p. 354)

The Black codes established staunch penalties for freedmen who sought to participate in southern society as equals. Ultimately, as an outcome of the laws, Black higher education was often a secret activity relegated to the backwoods and conducted over logs of wood by candlelight. A slave named Papa Dallas recounted to his granddaughter his ordeal stating the following:

> When I was young, just about your age, I used to steal away under a big oak tree and I tried to learn my alphabets so that I could learn to read my bible. But one day the overseer caught me and he drug me out on the plantation and he called out for all the field hands. And he turned to 'em and said, "let this be a lesson to all of you darkies. You ain't got no right to learn to read!" And then, daughter, he whooped me, and he whooped me, and he whooped me. And daughter, as if that wasn't enough, he turned around and he burned my eyes out! (Berlin, Favreau, Miller, & Kelley, 1998, p. 281)

Despite the danger, African Americans persisted in pursuit of literacy. Slaves, who were successful in acquiring an education, often gained their freedom. Frederick Douglass remarks in a speech delivered on October 1841 in Lynn, Massachusetts, on behalf of the Anti-Slavery Society: "A large portion of slaves know that they have a right to their liberty—it is often talked about and read of, for some of us know how to read, although all our knowledge is gained in secret" (Wright, 2009, p. 194).

The slave narratives suggest that being educated by their liberal masters, or escapees who were self-taught, education in the 19th century was a sought-after commodity. These narratives from slaves who were either educated by their liberal masters or escapees are proof that education was a coveted commodity among African-American communities. The growing sentiment at this time was the belief that education would improve quality of life (Tillman, 2009, p. 23).

Given that the aforementioned historical literature are primary sources, this study sets out to provide valuable insight into freedmen's conviction that literacy was important to the future of the race. Secondly, it is sensitive to the vehement opposition to Black literacy by southern planters through the issuance of state laws to prohibit the flourishing of Black education.

Significance of the Study

This study will secure a unique place in the existing literature because of the dearth of comparative historical research projects, which provide a comparison of two Black colleges that embody the diversity of Black higher education in the United States. Also, no study has been found that compared the first founding presidents of Black higher educational institutions founded by religious denominations during Reconstruction in the United States. It will thus contribute to the academic literature about the history of Black education in the United States, more specifically the prototype of leadership and infrastructure which makes historically Black colleges and universities (HBCU) successful. Moreover, it may be used as a reference book for current presidents and administrators of these institutions.

This study is significant for four major reasons. First, to date this writer has found no comparative historical research project conducted that compares two Black colleges that embody the diversity of Black higher education in the United States, as found in Wilberforce University and Morehouse College. This study makes a significant contribution to the corpus of research on Black higher education.

Second, no study has been found that compared the first founding presidents of Black higher educational institutions founded by religious denominations during Reconstruction in the United States. Mbajekwe (2009) observes that the prevailing literature overlooks the views and leadership of men and women who have led Black institutions in scholarly discussions about American higher education (p. 3).

This type of historical analysis is thus needed to elaborate the leadership strategies that these founding presidents developed to meet the needs of their respective institutions approximately 150 years ago. Accordingly, this study makes a significant contribution to research available on the educational leadership of Black higher educational institutions in the United States.

The third contribution of this research project is its account of the impacts of the social, economic, and political forces in the liberal North and the conservative South on the success of Black higher educational institutions. This study provides both, a unique historical glimpse into the founding of Black colleges and a complete analysis of how these institutions responded to local, regional, and national issues of 19th century United States. In doing so, it is sensitive to how these Black colleges dealt with various issues that still affect contemporary institutions and the African-American community. Finally, this study is central in virtue of its analysis of the early evolution of Black colleges, in showing the symbiosis of their development, organization, and institutional structure, public and private resources, and sponsorship.

Summary

Through the accomplishments of Bishop Payne and President Robert, each college made distinct impacts on Black higher education in the following areas: (a) the preparation of religious leadership, (b) the shaping of Black identity, and (c) the creation of a Black middle class. This study provides insight into their presidential tenures by comparing and contrasting their leadership approach and styles. The goal is that this research will assist contemporary Black colleges as they face similar challenges in their ongoing development. Furthermore, this study adds to the knowledge in the field of educational leadership and management.

2

Historical Methodology

This chapter outlines the historical method and approach to this study. This chapter defines and explains the selection of scientific management as the educational theory underpinning this study. It also defines and explains the use of Dr. Jim Laub's servant leadership *organizational leadership assessment* (OLA) model. (Is there any connection between scientific management and Laub's model, which should be mentioned?) This chapter, also, details the historical research methodologies used to establish protocols for data collection, processing, and interpretation.

Methodology

Historical Research

As in any discipline of social science there are numerous methods, approaches, and tools used to guide research investigation. The historical field uses these resources as well. In fact, historical methods have evolved more rapidly than any other social science, given that it is the most influenced by the methodological advancements of its sister fields (Znaniecki,

Not For Ourselves Alone, pages 17–31
Copyright © 2019 by Information Age Publishing

17

1952, p. 113). Accordingly, this study takes the necessary steps to define the terms that guide its approach to the topic.

Definition of Terms

What is history? According to David Krathwohl (1998), history is an academic discipline consisting of the discovery, selection, organization, and interpretation of evidence to describe a situation or to answer a question about past events (p. 571). What are historical methods? Distinguishing history as a consideration of specific content, Krathwohl (1998) maintains that its methods include careful and sometimes clever application of logic and basic social science research techniques (p. 571). These techniques include the following: understanding how to use research to inform the study, identify and isolate variables, determine appropriate resource identification and utilization methods, evaluate scientific material, and identify and utilize new resources for information gathering. The definition of historical research that will be used for this study is that historical research is the process by which various historical matter are evaluated, authenticated, and applied to content. This is a good place to state how you will apply this model of historical research to the specific content of this study and the results that it will yield.

Method and Approach

The above historical research techniques and historical model will be applied to the historical research of Black higher education during Reconstruction in the United States through methodical consideration of the historical and cultural contexts in which Wilberforce University and Morehouse College were founded. It gathers various evidences and artifacts to present qualitative interpretation, analysis, and narrative of the topic in order to answer the five research questions identified in Chapter 1. The application of the historical model and historical research technique is carried out through the elaboration of a complete historiography of Reconstruction, which draws out the cultural ground of 19th century African-American communities. This reinterpretation is key to conducting a historical research project that places African-American communities at the center of U.S. Reconstruction history. This approach is often used by Barzun and Graff (1985), who hold that "the past cannot help but be reconceived by every generation, but the earlier reports upon it are as good and true as they ever were. The picture is never finished, more recent accounts are not necessarily more true, each subtracts a little and adds more" (p. 191). This approach will be referred to as historical "mini-narratives."

Historical Mini-Narratives

The in-depth historiography of the critical issues and debates that shaped the political climate of the 19th century through the following historical mini-narratives: The Republican Party and the Beginning of Reconstruction; The Beginnings of Reconstruction in the South; The Failure of Self Reconstruction, 1865–1867; The Union League and Freedmen's Bureau and Reconstruction; Unionists and Scalawags; Community Perspectives; Comparative Perspectives; Black Labor; The Role of Violence; Religion and Reconstruction in the North; and The Constitutional Legacy of Reconstruction.

This section identifies the following critical issues: post-Civil War reunification of the North (Union) and South (Confederacy), endurance of federalist ideology (one nation under God politics), protection of the natural and civil rights of Southern loyalists and former confederates, protection of the natural and civil rights of former slaves and their descendants, transition from an agricultural to an industrial economy, role of the federal government in protecting the civil rights of citizens, and protection of states' rights. We shall now consider data source selection and the construction of mini-narratives.

Data Collection, Authentication, and Analysis

This project adheres diligently to the three essential steps in the production of historical research, namely, the gathering of the data; the criticism of the data; and the presentation of facts, interpretations, and conclusions in readable form (Hockett, 1970, p. 9). By adhering to these essential steps, the goal is to achieve exemplar scholarship, which may inform future research in this field.

The fact that historians cannot manipulate treatment, create new data, or take new measures constitutes the first step of data collection. Historians are bound by the artifacts and records that they've inherited (Krathwohl, 1998, p. 577). In compliance with this step, this study focuses on the identification of all primary source materials available, while being sensitive to their context. These sources include the following: board of director minutes; newspaper articles/announcements; state charters and incorporation documents; presidential speeches and other related published works; and college newspapers, bulletins, and other artifacts.

Moreover, quality data collection depends upon the historian's access to the best libraries and use of collections that have a variety of materials, catalogues, indexes, and aids to support the research. For meritorious production must rest largely on sources (Hockett, 1970, p. 89). The author of this study was granted access and used various libraries, archives, and special collections dedicated to the study of Black higher education at Wilberforce University and Morehouse College. The resources and pertinent artifacts at these libraries provided the necessary data to answer the research questions.

The second step in data authentication is identified by historians as internal and external criticism. Internal criticism consists of the process of establishing the accuracy or worth of data collected and external criticism takes up the authentication of artifacts (Krathwohl, 1998, p. 578). In this study, the process of internal criticism is carried out in the data collection step, as primary sources have been authenticated by the libraries that hold them in certified collections.

The process of external criticism is carried out by applying Garraghan's (1946) model for the authenticity of sources. Garraghan notes that external criticism is a complex process that involves six distinct inquiries: (a) "When was the source produced (date)?"; (b) "Where was it produced (localization)?"; (c) "By whom was it produced (authorship)?"; (d) "From what pre-existing material was it produced (analysis)?"; (e) "In what original form was it produced (integrity)?"; and, (f) "What is the eventual value of its contents (credibility)?" (Garraghan, 1946, p. 168). This study ensures that each source meets this criterion.

The third step data in analysis bears two criteria. First, historians must possess the historical mindedness needed to interpret the data. Historical mindedness is closely related to semantic, hermeneutic, textual criticism, empathy, or intuition. The best definition is the historians' ability to suspend his/her own preconceptions and to take on his subjects in the effort to understand the latter's language, ideals, interests, attitudes, habits, motives, drives, and traits (Gottschalk, 1969, p. 137). Through a rigorous investigation of its research questions, this study approaches data analysis by applying the aforementioned definition of historical mindedness to provide a historical account of the educational experience of African Americans in the United States during Reconstruction.

This study is particularly sensitive to the leadership styles and visions of Presidents Payne and Robert in Chapter 4; it provides an account of their efforts as pioneer leaders in devising HBCUs as the suitable institutions to educate African Americans. Second, the historian must satisfy the conditions to draw causation by ensuring that the rationale or explanation plays the same role in historical studies as in others (Krathwohl, 1998, p. 582). Chapters 5 and 6 fulfill the conditions for drawing causation by identifying changes in causes and the corresponding change in effects that occurred in response to the multiple social, cultural, political, and economic forces that led to the founding of Wilberforce University and Morehouse College.

Theory of Education and Community Leadership

Theories of education and community leadership center on the following key concepts: (a) maintenance of stability and order in the social system, (b) use of biological organism as a metaphor, and (c) the necessity of society's adaptive mechanisms to ensure survival. Close attention to the evolution of social systems through their states of equilibrium reveals that their leadership use shared norms and values to legitimize human participation and institutionalize behavior through social functions. Furthermore, this theory considers culture as an integrated body of knowledge, pseudo-knowledge, beliefs, and values through which human life is lived (Coppola, 2005, p. 32).

During the early 20th century, functionalism was applied to the effective management of industrial organizations. From this, functionalism has mostly influenced the field of educational leadership through the theory of scientific management, as it delineates the link between purpose and management (Bush, 1999, p. 240). The process through which social systems, as organizations, work to increase the productivity of individuals and the outputs of the collective is particularly relevant. Thus, we must consider the works of Frederick W. Taylor and Henri Fayol in the development of scientific management and its principles. Given that the primary objective of Black colleges has been and remains to increase the social and intellectual capital of African Americans the aims of the first Black colleges were thus similar to other social systems and organizations of the time period, that is, to increase social capital by improving modes of production. This study also considers the works of Booker T. Washington and W. E. B. Du Bois to provide a social and scientific analysis of the purposes of these institutions.

Taylor's Scientific Management

An important contribution to the development of scientific management was made by Frederick W. Taylor. An engineer by trade, Taylor in the early

19th century sought to increase the efficiency and effectiveness of industrial organizations (factories) through a qualitative and quantitative assessment of: (a) the relationships developed between managers and workers, (b) the relationships developed between workers within their specializations, and (c) the relationship developed between the worker and his/her valuation of work tasks. In his address to the Cleveland Advertising Club on March 3, 1915, Taylor makes the following remarks:

> The one great thing that marks the improvement of this world is measured by the enormous increase in output of the individuals in this world. There is fully twenty times the output per man now than there was three hundred years ago. That marks the increase in the real wealth of the world; that marks the increase of the happiness of the world, that gives us the opportunity for shorter hours, for better education, for amusement, for art, for music, for everything that is worthwhile in this world... (Shafritz, 2005, p. 62)

Singularly, Taylor (1911) in his work, *The Principles of Scientific Management*, measures social progress in terms of the ability of individuals to increase the outputs (profit) of an organization. Taylor (1911) defines scientific management as the outcome of a revolution of the employer's and worker's consciousness In Taylor's mind, scientific management is twofold. It occurs once the employer changes his/her outlook towards their duty, themselves, and workers, and the workers transform their outlook upon themselves and their employers. Taylor in his speech to advertisers articulates the mental revolution necessary to precede the increase of profit in organizations and factories:

> The new outlook that comes under scientific management is this: The workmen, after many object lessons, come to see and the management come to see that this surplus can be made so great, providing both sides will stop, their pulling apart, will stop their fighting and will push as hard as they can to get as cheap an output as possible, that there is no occasion to quarrel. Each side can get more than ever before. The acknowledgement of this fact represents a complete mental revolution. (Shafritz, 2005, p. 65)

As theorized by Taylor (1911), progress is a process through which managers support workers to find innovative ways to increase their productivity. This process is then identified as scientific management. To ensure that progress occurs, Taylor outlines the following four principles of scientific management: (a) Managers must make an earnest endeavor to end soldiering by making it unnecessary for workers to deceive management; (b) managers must voluntarily take on the task of gathering worker's practical knowledge, creating—science (rules, laws, and mathematical formulae) to apply this knowledge through work habits (motion study) and efficient use of time spent on tasks (time study); (c) Managers must be scientific about their selection of workers, while also providing a means for their growth and development through training; and (d) Managers must be involved in the complete redivision of the work of the establishment, in order to create a sense of real cooperation with the workers (Shafritz, 2005, pp. 63–67).

The author's incentive for assessing the theoretical contributions of Taylor (1911) to organizational theory through his principles of scientific management is to assess how social systems as organizations function to increase the productivity of individuals. Moreover, Taylor's organizational theory sheds light on how organizations operate to increase the outputs of the collective when both the organization and the individual are considered in relation to their changing environment. Thus, we must consider the work of Henri Fayol.

Fayol's Process of Management

Fayol's (1916) *General Principles of Management,* is considered as a classic in the literature about scientific management. In this text, Fayol contextualizes the function of management within an organization as a responsibility for "maintaining the soundness and good working order of the body corporate" (Fayol, 1916, p. 19). Constance Storrs observes that Fayol's greatest contribution to management was his identification of the organization as a "body corporate." In her translation of Fayol's *General and Industrial Management* work:

> Fayol's term—corps social, meaning all those engaged in a given corporate activity in any sphere, is best rendered by this somewhat unusual term because (a) it retains his implied biological metaphor; (b) it represents the structure as distinct from the process of organization. The term will be retained in all contexts where these two requirements have to be met. (Storrs, as cited in Shafritz, 2005, p. 60)

It is common knowledge that the use of biological metaphors in organizational theories are bedrocks of functionalism. However, Fayol (1916) is the first to embed practices and guidelines for increased effectiveness in management by emphasizing the necessity to study management as a dynamic process. Furthermore, the managerial insights of Fayol are unique given that he bases their selection on success in praxis and application. Fayol thinks that this set of principles is indispensable. In his words:

> Whether a case of commerce, industry, politics, religion, war, or philanthropy, in every concern there is a management function to be performed, and for its performance there must be principles, that is to say acknowledged truths regarded as proven on which to rely. And it is the code which represents the sum total of these truths at any given moment. (Fayol, 1916, p. 42)

For Fayol, the most important aspect of management is the ways in which individuals in organizations collaborate to achieve goals and objectives. Fayol (1916) sought to ascertain key factors, or indicators that are conducive to organizational harmony. Emphasizing the role of management in leading and guiding the planning of work activities, Fayol outlines 14 principles and objectives for effective management: (a) division of work—acquire an ability, sureness, and accuracy to increase outputs, (b) authority and responsibility—provide workers with the appropriate directives, (c) discipline—maintain a code of conduct, (d) unity of command—set clear reporting structures, (e) unity of direction—ensure one person outlines a single vision and plan, (f) subordination of individual interest to general interest—ensure that the interest of one employee or group does not supersede the interest of the organization as a whole, (g) remuneration of personnel—maintain equity in employee compensation, (h) centralization—optimize use of all faculties, (i) scalar chain—reconcile respect for chain of command and need for swift action, (j) order—acquire balance between human requirements and resources, (k) equity—treat each worker with kindliness and justice, (l) stability of tenure of personnel—afford management time to form relationships and skills that lead to success, (m) initiative—engage managers in thoughtful design of a plan, and (n) esprit de corps—create a culture that considers the importance of harmony in the work environment (Shafritz, 2005, pp. 48–59).

Booker T. Washington and W. E. B. Du Bois on Black Education

The issue of the best approach to educate Black children has been the topic of debate since the late 18th century. The attempt to elaborate the most suitable approach to educate Black children shapes the infrastructure of Black higher education, as well. Historians have observed tensions in theories of Black higher education over the issue of how best to invest in Black children, ensuring the future viability of the race. The attempt to elaborate the most effective strategy to educate African-American communities is exemplified through the liberal arts and religious education institutions founded between 1850 and 1870. In the model of the shift to agricultural and industrial focused institutions being founded between 1870 and 1910,

Black higher education was often viewed as the means to increase Black social capital and to transform the Southern economy from a dependence on slave labor to a more skilled workforce (Bullock, 1970, p. 165).

Early historians of freedmen's education argued that a major motivation for Northern activism was economic (Anderson & Moss, 1999, pp. 1–3). As the Civil War came to a triumphant end for the Union, Northern industrialists saw an opportunity to reshape U.S. import/export markets by investing in black consumerism. While Southern planters attempted to maintain control of Black labor by opposing Black education, Northern businessmen invested heavily into the Black education movement. As a result, the White leaders of aid societies and religious denominations were often businessmen and manufactures. They assumed that educated men and women had greater material appetites and would buy Northern products to satiate them. The hope thus emerged that Southern Black schooling would open new markets and was seen as the most important reason for the education of Negros (Butchart, 1980, p. 56).

Within this paradigm, education as social responsibility is often equated with race consciousness. Even though, Northerners participated in building Black educational institutions, but their incentive is ambiguous: Was it the liberation and betterment of the Black race? Or the production of a new working class? The role of Black higher education during post-Civil War and Reconstruction would most vigorously be debated in Booker T. Washington's (1901) *Up From Slavery* and W. E. B. Du Bois' (1903) *The Talented Tenth*. Even though, they are often characterized as oppositional Black political and educational theorists, Washington (1901) and Du Bois (1903), their debate represents an important period of critical reflection on how African Americans should take advantage and advocate for additional social, political, and economic resources. The core issue for Washington and Dubois is the development of Black social capital within the context of a quality Black higher education model. Washington expresses this belief in the following statement:

> In our [Tuskegee Institute] industrial teaching we keep three things in mind: first, that the student shall be so educated that he shall be enabled to meet conditions as they exist now, in the part of the South where he lives—in a word, to be able to do the thing which the world wants done; second, that every student who graduates from the school shall have enough skill coupled with intelligence and moral character, to enable him to make a living for himself and others; third, to send every graduate out feeling and knowing that labour is dignified and beautiful—to make each one love labour instead of trying to escape it. (as cited in Wright, 2009, p. 401)

Du Bois summarizes his perspective in the statement below:

The Negro race, like all races, is going to be saved by its exceptional men. The problem of education, then, among Negroes must first of all deal with the Talented Tenth; it is the problem of developing the Best of the race that they may guide the Mass away from the contamination and death of the Worst, in their own and other races. (as cited in Wright, 2009, p. 410)

As educational visionaries, Washington (1901) and Du Bois (1903) offer unique outlooks on the significance of Black higher education, specifically, its implication for the larger discussions of the time period on the philosophical, political, social, moral, and economic destinies of African-American communities. They agreed that education was the arena in which the critical issues facing the United States in the development of the New South's capitalist and market economy and its impact on educated ex-slaves would be determined. They also agreed that the purpose of Black higher education was to create a new Black elite, rather than a new working class proposed by Northerners. However, Washington and Du Bois disagreed on the role higher educational institutions played in areas of increasing productivity, reliability, and profitability of the Black work force. The crux of their debate is how Black higher educational institutions must elaborate an educational model to elevate slaves into doctors, actors, and businessmen who are equipped to enjoy full citizenship.

Du Bois (1929) offers a philosophical understanding of how African Americans, during Reconstruction, felt about these emerging capitalist and market economies in the New South, and their influence on race relations and empowerment of freedmen. Du Bois commented that "economic power underlies politics ... they did not know that when they let the dictatorship of labor be overthrown in the South they surrendered the hope of democracy in America for all men." (pp. 591–592). He then argued that "the espousal of the doctrine of Negro inferiority by the South was primarily because of economic motives and the inter-connected political urge necessary to support slave industry..." (p. 39). In Du Bois (1938) the education of African Americans is dependent upon their commitment to constantly reflect on their freedoms in the context of their own communal ideals and institutions (as cited in Aptheker, 1973, p. 118). Governmental freedom in a capitalistic society is measured by one's ability to increase and actualize potential for self-realization through access to various social resources. Granting freedom is indeed a governmental investment of resources with the expectation that a product of value would be gained in return. In a basic sense, society, in capitalistic economies, operates as the context for the participation in the freedom of production (Aptheker, 1973, pp. 123–124).

This was the major issue in Reconstruction Georgia, North Carolina, and Tennessee, the freedom of African-Americans was a license to participate in production. Freedom presumed that the freed individual maintains the right to invest his/her resources into the purchase of commodities that brings them closer to their desired goal. This quasi-agriculturalist system of harvesting (modes of production) has been defined, philosophically, as laissez-faire liberalism. This perception, of modes of production, views society as a field of investigation (experiment) in addition to the individual and the state, each adhering to certain laws of self-regulating competition (Skirbekk & Gilje, 2001, p. 266).

In this context Black higher educational institutions are responsible for ensuring that African Americans remain a community of stakeholders in the economy of freedom, a participant in the American experiment, or a co-investor with a similar vision/goal for the future (Aptheker, 1973, p. 95). Du Bois (1933) concludes that the university must train the children of a nation for life and for making a living, becoming a perfect expression of the center of the intellectual and cultural expression of its age (Aptheker, 1973, p. 88). Essentially, Black higher educational institutions must create leaders, and even more specifically servant leaders who understand the importance of Black education and how to equip young people with the skills, tools, and competencies to assume leadership positions in this capitalist and agriculturalist system.

Laub's Organizational Leadership Assessment Model

Revisiting Taylor (1911) one can begin to redefine the role of transformation in the shaping of quality leadership. Since Downton's (1973) coinage of the term transformational leadership and James MacGregor Burns (1978) use of transformation to define a leader's attempt to motivate followers towards a goal, the role of transformation (or simply radical change) in leadership has often been characterized by one's ability to bring about a change within others; or the ability to motivate persons to bring change to their environment. Northouse (2004) defines transformational leadership as the process whereby an individual engages with others and creates a connection that raises the level of motivation and morality in both the leader and the follower (p. 170). However, there is room in these definitions to question the role of change within an organization, as a unique entity endowed with a specific goal. The best way to understand leadership is to view it as a means to revolutionize the purpose and mission of a given organization.

As mentioned above, the use of scientific management by university administrators and the academy-at-large marked a historical period when the practices of leadership as a determinant of institutional effectiveness received much attention. With Washington's (1901) and Du Bois's (1933) increased focus on the complexities of quality leadership in Black higher education, this study frames a response to the anomaly faced by administrators, specifically regarding how educational organizations were affected by social, economic, and political change in the United States during Reconstruction.

Furthermore, in light of the Du Boisian view of Black higher education, administrators realized by the late 19th to the mid-20th century that social progress was not predicated upon change among the workers and followers alone; rather, raising academic quality depended upon critical reflection on the leadership and mission of colleges and universities in the United States. The winning formula posited that sustained management and study of change would lead to intellectual progress. The critical question is: If the quality of leadership is the most important element in the production of a quality college or university, then what are the important variables, incidents, and/or circumstances that result in the reproduction of quality amongst all Black higher educational institutions.

An important dimension of this study is the data collection and analysis of artifacts that uncover Presidents Payne and Robert's leadership styles. Comparing and contrasting their leadership dynamics, Chapter 5 of this study further analyzes each president's impact on their respective institutions. Situating Wilberforce University and Morehouse College in their specific historical context, this study assesses the aforementioned research questions and any emergent historical problems. The theoretical framework chosen to guide this analysis is Dr. James Alan Laub's (2000) Organizational Leadership Assessment.

Dr. Laub (2000) in his paper, "The Development of the Organizational Leadership Assessment (OLA) Model," uses servant leadership as a theoretical foundation of the ideal leadership strategy. Servant leadership is an organizational leadership theory developed by Robert Greenleaf (1970) to specify the difference between a leader that emerges from within or without the group to assume authority, in contrast to a leader that uses servant characteristics, such as caring, morality, active listening, and mentoring, while deriving power from their followers to emerge as the authority within the group. Greenleaf's account of servant leadership is not particularly popular. However, the premise of servant leadership is that the leader is one who seeks to serve and serving is a natural component of the leader (Farling, Stone, & Winston, 1999; Greenleaf, 1977).

Laub's (2000) research goal is to help define servant leadership in terms of its characteristics in order to use those characteristics to design an assessment tool that can be used within organizations to detect the presence of those characteristics (p. 4). Laub's characterization of servant organizations is central to this study. The servant organization is defined here as an organization where the characteristics of servant leadership are displayed through organizational culture in which they are valued and practiced by its leadership and workforce (Laub, 2000, p. 24). Laub makes the following observation regarding this new concept:

> The term servant organization is not found in the literature, though Greenleaf spoke of the institution as servant. Greenleaf, however, addressed the organizational issues involved rather than the idea of assessing an organization in light of the characteristics of servant leadership. This author believes that the servant organization is a natural extension and application of the concept of servant leadership. (p. 23)

Colleges and universities in general are social organisms, and therefore products of their larger cultural environments. Colleges and universities are created to fulfill the educational needs of specific populations; these needs shape colleges and universities' mission, purpose, vision, commitment, and most important leadership style.

TABLE 2.1   Laub's (2000) Organizational Leadership Model

Servant Leader Value	Servant Organization Value
Values People	• Believing in people • Fulfilling others' needs before his or her own • Practicing receptive and nonjudgmental listening
Develops People	• Providing opportunities for learning and growth • Modeling appropriate behavior • Encouraging and affirming others by praising their talents
Builds Community	• Building strong personal relationships • Working collaboratively with others • Acknowledging and tolerating the different views of others
Displays Authenticity	• Remaining open and accountable to others • Displaying willingness to learn from others • Maintaining integrity and trust
Provides Leadership	• Envisioning the future • Taking initiative • Clarifying goals
Shares Leadership	• Developing a shared vision • Sharing power and releasing control • Sharing status and promoting others

Close attention to Dr. Payne and Dr. Joseph's leadership styles depicts servant characteristics, such as caring, morality, active listening, and mentoring, while deriving power from their followers to emerge as the authority within the group. Under the light of their leadership, Black colleges during Reconstruction in the United States, fit in Laub's (2000) definition of a servant organization. Furthermore, leadership of any higher educational institution requires: (a) a willingness to cope with a unique set of challenges, transforming them into organizational success; (b) an openness of all stakeholders to personal and institutional transformation; (c) a willingness of all stakeholders to expand their knowledge and understanding of the higher education institution's community; and (d) a leadership team which is driven by the conviction to pursue the higher education institution's mission despite the opposition and obstacles that may arise. These principles match the servant leadership profile used in the OLA model. Moreover, applying Laub's (2000) model to this study provides an assessment framework that measures the historical impact of leadership characteristics on the institution within its time period and the present.

Limitation of the Study

Every research project has inherent limitations and historical research has a specific set. The limitations of this study are lack of access to the methods used to authenticate primary sources, lack of research on the founding presidents of Black colleges, and lack of living subjects. It is an unfortunate fact that archives for such a study which date back over 150 years are often limited in quality and quantity. Unfortunately, many of the artifacts preserved during this time period at the college and university did not survive. In the case of Wilberforce, the fire of 1865 destroyed many of the artifacts this study would have utilized. In the case of Morehouse, a single history of the Atlanta Baptist Seminary still exists from that time period. Additionally, this study is concerned primarily with the leadership style of the founder of each college. This study provides the history of Wilberforce University and Morehouse College until 1884. This limitation is due to the unavailability of living persons available for interview.

Lastly, given that it is required that researchers indicate how their historical and social backgrounds influence the research project, the author of this study is the son of two African Methodist Episcopal Church ministers and was a member of this denomination for 19 years. Additionally, the author is a graduate of Morehouse College. These factors reinforce the need to maintain objectivity and to acknowledge that perspectives from firsthand experiences do not extend to the time period studied. Though, the research and findings are the outcome of careful attention to rigorous methodology, to ensure the judicious reconstruction of events and interpretation of their impact on the historical time period studied.

3

Historical Context

This chapter provides a deeper account of the various social, economic, political, and racial forces that led to the founding of Wilberforce University and Morehouse College during Reconstruction in the United States. Its aim is to develop the thesis that Black education during Reconstruction was the natural implication of a pre-existing struggle for African-American self-improvement and community empowerment.

The Development of Black Higher Education

Chapter 1 claims that the roots of Black higher education are: Black desire for literacy, Black motivation for self and communal empowerment, and the goal of White Northerners to create Black consumer markets. This history is divided into three historical time periods. The first covers the history of Black higher education from slavery to emancipation (c1562–c1863). The second covers the history of Black higher education post-emancipation to the civil rights era (c1864–c1965). The third covers the history of Black

Not For Ourselves Alone, pages 33–64
Copyright © 2019 by Information Age Publishing

higher education post-civil rights era to the present (c1966–present). This chapter will focus on the rise of Black higher education in the United States.

The second period in the development of Black higher education begins with President Abraham Lincoln's Emancipation Proclamation of April 1863, and may be characterized as an educational golden age for African Americans. This period is considered a golden age because it reflects unprecedented educational entrepreneurship by freed people. Cynthia Jackson and Eleanor F. Nunn (2003) note that of the 103 historically Black colleges and universities (HBCUs) currently operating, approximately 75% of them were established between 1865 and 1899. In addition, over 90% of the HBCUs were created in the South. Such a large percentage of HBCUs in the South is the outcome of the exclusion of African Americans from White institutions in the North and South (p. 3).

The Black church also played a major role in sponsoring schools for ex-slaves. One Freedmen's Bureau superintendent of education in Kentucky said in 1867: "The places of worship owned by the colored people are almost the only available school houses in the state" (Anderson, 1998, p. 13). As such, the literature produced by these organizations is critical to an understanding of Black higher education. Moreover, it is proof of the dual role of the Black church in African-American communities, as a spiritual haven and socio-educational institution.

The most salient expression of this dual role of the Black church is illustrated in the accomplishments of Bishop Daniel Alexander Payne. Bishop Payne assumed the dual roles of pastor and publisher of pamphlets. Eventually, as a founding trustee of Wilberforce University of the Methodist Church in 1850, he became its first Black president in 1865. In the following statement, Bishop Payne emphasizes the importance of education to the development of the race:

> But of the children take special care. Heaven has entrusted them to you for a special purpose. What is that purpose? Not merely to eat and to drink, still less to gormandize. Not merely to dress finely in broadcloths, silks, satins, jewelry, nor to dance to the sound of tambourine and fiddle; but to learn them how to live and how to die—to train them for great usefulness on earth—to prepare them for great glory in heaven. Keep your children in the schools, even if you have to eat less, drink less and wear coarser raiment; though you eat but two meals a day, purchase but one change of garment during the year. . . . Let the education of your children penetrate the heart. (Sernett, 1985, p. 220)

Bishop Payne's reflections above represent an emergence of the sentiment that education is a social and moral obligation of parents toward their children. Moreover, investing in one's children's education is conducive to the future viability of the race. Within this paradigm, education as a social responsibility is often equated with race consciousness. Representatives of this genre of literature in Black higher education included Booker T. Washington (1901) and W. E. B. Du Bois (1903). Washington and Dubois are, thus, akin to Bishop Payne and Dr. Joseph in the common endeavor of devising the most suitable strategies to educate African-American communities post-emancipation.

The third historical time period of Black higher education begins with the signing of the Civil Rights Act in 1965 by President Lyndon B. Johnson. This period is characterized by scholarship that seeks to build on the educational theories developed in the previous time periods. Hallmarks of this scholarship are that of A. J. Jaffe, Walter Adams, and Sandra G. Meyers' (1968) who conducted a study, *Negro Higher Education in the 1960's,* and Henry Allen Bullock's (1970), *A History of Negro Education in the South.* Bullock (1970) based his work on the presupposition that the educational and social revolution of his modern day was never intended, rather, developed out of liberating responses elicited by the nation's efforts to maintain the status quo.

The education of African Americans in the South repeatedly served as the main leverage for this movement. And despite purposeful efforts to the contrary, it has been pushing the movement toward the complete emancipation of the Negro American as a person (Bullock, 1970, p. xv). Jaffe et al. (1968) carried out a similar study, which focused exclusively on Southern Negro colleges and their students. Their quantitative research model attempted to draw out the statistics of the causes of Black students' success at Southern HBCUs. Bullock (1970) is primarily concerned with the historical development of educational opportunities for African Americans in the South and how these evolving opportunities facilitated the desegregation movement in the United States (Jaffe et. al., 1968, pp. v–viii, xiii).

The genealogy of Black higher education's study is rooted in Bullock's (1970) view that education is a subject for ethnographic research. As such, it laid the foundation for the authorship of historical case studies on Black higher education in the North and South during and after Reconstruction. Ethnographic studies of Black higher education include: Leonard Meece's (1932) *Negro Education in Kentucky*; Richard J. Roche's dissertation entitled, *Catholic Colleges and the Negro Student*; Lillian Dabney's (1949) dissertation, *The History of Schools for Negroes in the District of Columbia, 1807–1947*; Frederick A. McGinnis (1962), *The Education of Negroes in Ohio*; J. Irving Scott's (1974) *The Education of Black People in Florida*; and the previously quoted Ronald E. Butchart's (1980), *Northern Schools, Southern Blacks, and Reconstruction.*

A classic in ethnographic studies of Black higher education is *The Education of Blacks in the South, 1860–1935* published by James D. Anderson in 1998. It is considered as the most significant historical case study of Black higher education entitled, *The Education of Blacks in the South, 1860–1935.* Therein, Anderson (1998) provides a thorough historical account of Black higher education that gives voice to the various slave narratives and other primary source materials. This approach pioneered a new approach to the historiography of Black higher education, which is centered on uncovering African-Americans' motivations, methods, and mechanisms for educating themselves and their children.

The study of Black higher education post-Civil Rights, also, focused on how higher education in general, and Black colleges specifically, effectively prepared young people to be leaders in their communities. Furthermore, it grants them the necessary intellectual capital to research and respond effectively to critical issues facing African-American communities. Interest in this type of historical research on Black higher education is best defined as a history of the role and function of colleges and universities in African-American communities, the nation, and the world. This genre flourished in response to DuBois' (1909) critique of the Hampton model, and DuBois' (1933) publication, *The Field and Function of the Negro College,* in which he radically opposed new Negro college presidents' attempt to secularize their institutions, deemphasizing their cultural heritage (Aptherker, 1973, p. 83).

Historiography of Reconstruction: An Unsettling Political Climate

Reconstruction was as a defining moment in the life of a nation engaged in the process of re-envisioning the ideals espoused by its founding fathers in the U.S. Constitution; this process left lasting effects on its political, social, and economic practices post-Civil War and post-emancipation. Fitzgerald (2007) considers the political climate of 19th century United States as the most dominant force in determining the success or failure of Reconstruction. He clarifies the historical significance of Reconstruction, which he regards as a process of negotiating the reunification of the states, at the heart of which was the appeasement of the political, social, and economic concerns of the Southern Christian democrat plantation owning middle class (p. x). According to Fitzgerald's approach, the political, social, and economic climate, which shaped 19th century United States stems from Civil War and emancipation, as independent yet interconnected historical events.

The aforementioned point is often lost in the fog of historical accounts offered by conservative constructivists and liberal deconstructionists. The actors in the Reconstruction drama in the United States were often torn between their desires to rebuild the nation and to re-envision the role of freedmen in American society. Any historiography of Reconstruction which fails to acknowledge this fact is short sighted. Furthermore, an analysis of the 19th century's political climate and the often contradictory views held by many of the actors is mandatory to provide a broad historical account of the Reconstruction.

Reconstruction begins with President Abraham Lincoln's issuance of the Emancipation Proclamation in 1863, an executive order that freed slaves in the Confederate states, and ends with the presidential election of 1876, in which Rutherford B. Hayes was elected as the 19th President of the United States, contingent upon the withdrawal of federal troops from the South. Regarding the presidential election of 1876, Fitzgerald (2007) writes: "[Rutherford B. Hayes] did not consciously betray black rights; he instead indulged in an optimistic scenario to ease retreat from an impossible situation" (p. 207). Fitzgerald's reflection on the election of 1876 is an illustration of the reality of the aforementioned struggles of the nation's executive branch to develop an effective political agenda in order to address all the concerns of the American people, specifically republicans and democrats in Congress. Some of these concerns were the reconstruction of Southern economy, Black suffrage, and the political empowerment and representation of freed Blacks and former Confederates nationally.

Historical Mini-Narratives

Identifying and determining the clear historical roots of the animosity between the Northern republican, federalist, industrialist, and Southern Democrat, confederate, planter during Reconstruction is no easy task. The six factors, given previously, provide an historical footprint and a general outline of ideological debates that shaped this period. These debates point to the urgent concern for racial tolerance and justice that defines the context and content of Reconstruction history in the United States. Unfortunately, previous historical accounts often avoid and/or decentralize the centrality of race in shaping American economics and politics during this time period and the following century (Belz, 1998, pp. 162–163). The historical account of Reconstruction in this project will situate the pursuit of racial tolerance and justice at the center of the North and South ideological debate and provide a review of the literature about Reconstruction in the United States.

Functioning as literary devices, the critical issues and debates that comprise the political climate of the 19th century Reconstruction era in the United States are told in the following historical mini-narratives: "The Republican Party and the Beginning of Reconstruction"; "The Beginnings of Reconstruction in the South"; "The Failure of Self Reconstruction During 1865–1867"; "The Union League, Freedmen's Bureau, and Reconstruction"; "Unionists and Scalawags"; "Community Perspectives"; "Comparative Perspectives"; "Black Labor"; "The Role of Violence"; "The North: Religion and Reconstruction"; and "The Constitutional Legacy." By revisiting each one of these mini-narratives, this section will deduce how the primary actors in the elaboration of Reconstruction addressed the following critical issues: the post-Civil War reunification of the North (Union) and South (Confederacy), the endurance of federalist ideology (one nation under God politics), the protection of the natural and civil rights of Southern loyalists and former confederates, the protection of the natural and civil rights of former slaves and their descendants, the transition from an agricultural to an industrial economy, the role of the federal government in protecting the natural and civil rights of citizens, and the protection of states' rights.

The Republican Party and the Beginning of Reconstruction

This historical mini-narrative is based on the ideological development of the Republican party at the beginning of Reconstruction. Herman Belz (2000) traces the evolution of emancipation from its beginning as a Northern social ideology into a component of the Republican party's political ideology, which is reflected in Lincoln's proclamation and executive order. It also attempts to reconstruct the history of the South during military reconstruction by drawing a link to its current state as a constitutional law. Belz (2000) emphasizes a major distinguishing factor of his research, namely, the principles and rules that embodied national civil rights policy depended on reflection, deliberation, and choice in the sphere of political philosophy and constitutionalism (p. viii). As such, Belz interprets emancipation as an outcome of a complicated process of political choice, action, and nonaction: "Motivated by pragmatic considerations rather than by concern for the slaves' personal liberty, they were content to declare the slaves of rebels free and to leave to future developments the determination of their status in the civil order" (p.14).

This mini-narrative raises the following question: "How did the Republican party work to further its Reconstruction ideology espoused by Lincoln, specifically, the reunification of the Union at all costs, while considering the protection of freedmen rights by the federal government?" This query leads to a political quandary. Republicans forged a Reconstruction agenda on the basis of the following two principles:

1. The political aims of Reconstruction should work towards guarding freedom versus enforcing equality.
2. Republicanism represented the necessity of constitutional equality, rather than equity amongst the races.

In his second inaugural speech on March 4, 1865, President Lincoln pronounced that

> with malice toward none, with charity for all, with firmness in the right as God gives us to see the right, let us strive on to finish the work we are in; to bind up the nation's wounds; to care for him who shall have borne the battle, and for his widow and his orphan—to do all which may achieve and cherish a just and lasting peace, among ourselves, and with all nations. (Abraham Lincoln's Second Inaugural Address, March 4, 1865, http://www.nationalcenter.org)

Belz (2000) notes that without abandoning the goal of laissez-faire legal equality, Republicans assumed the position that emancipated slaves need temporary guardianship (p. 71). To reunify the Union, post-emancipation, the federal government had to play a considerable role in protecting the rights of newly freedmen. However, for Republicans who held the majority in the Congress, the major question was: "To what extent should the federal government protect the rights of newly freedmen?" According to Belz's (2000) discussion of the development of the Freedmen's Bureau Legislation, the role of the federal government depended on the extent to which freedmen were believed to participate as citizens. If citizenship for former slaves granted access to constitutional freedom and privileges, then the responsibility for supporting their rights to access such freedom and privileges was a state issue, which could allow variance. However, if citizenship was a constitutional right extended to all equally and without difference, this right could not be mitigated by the states.

The rights of citizens are protected by the constitution and must be defended by the government. In reality, the beginning of Reconstruction was rooted in the debate over the future of freedmen. The Republican government leaned toward allowing freedmen independence to act as citizens, though temporary guardianship (adoption) was necessary to ensure that they could exercise these rights. This guardianship called for the creation of a central organization to oversee and manage the transition of freedmen from slaves to citizens. It thus became the onus of the Freedmen's Bureau to serve this purpose.

Additionally, Belz (2000) notes that the discrepancy between expectations in 1865 and 1866 concerning equality before the law reflected a failure to appreciate the depth and scope of the race question in the United States (p. 146). Unfortunately, 19th century Republicanism was incapable of fully embracing the opportunity presented by post-Civil War and post-emancipation to shape a new social reality in the United States. While the Republican party believed that freedmen should be allowed to exercise their full rights as citizens, they were unable to accept freedmen as their equals with the same level of social privileges. As such, they strived to protect the social privileges of White Southerners and their superiority over ex-slaves.

By 1862 the North and South had built powerful military machines. At the same time, the incentives of the North to go to war were shifting to include the abolition of slavery. The abolition of slavery implied the destruction of the Southern social and economic system. In the summer of 1862, the Lincoln administration adopted the radical Republican position that emancipation was a military necessity (Boydston et al., 2004, p. 353). Unwilling to challenge White supremacy in the South, Republicans negotiated a constitutional position that would influence political debate in each subsequent mini-narrative in order to preserve White supremacy. Nonetheless, as Belz (2000) explains, the efforts of the Republican party at the beginning of Reconstruction to introduce congressional legislation to protect freedmen's civil rights was a victory. It laid the foundation for future civil rights political activism and constitutional amendments.

The Beginnings of Reconstruction in the South

The history of the Roanoke Island freedmen's colony provides an interesting perspective on assessing the beginnings of Reconstruction. This colony serves as an exemplar of Black efforts to achieve self-reliance and sheds light on the social, political, and economic realities faced by Southern African-American communities, which were determined to attain civil rights through self-reliance.

Patricia C. Click (2001) provides a historical account of the development of the Roanoke Island colony in North Carolina's post the Battle of

Roanoke Island in 1862 to the evacuation of the colony.and declaration of amnesty by President Johnson in 1867. This historical account outlines: the pursuits of former slaves to define their social roles in Southern society, while managing their newly acquired freedom and the ensuing conflicts, which arose from the competing agendas of the American Missionary Association (AMA), the Union Military, the Freedmen's Bureau, the National Freedmen's Relief Association, and White landowners. As a precursor to Reconstruction, the experiences faced by these freedmen foreshadowed the later issues of the South.

Prior to Roanoke Island, the standard for meeting the needs of the freedmen was to gather them in camps controlled by the Union army and to provide temporary settlement until the government found a better solution. Under state control, these camps served only to provide freedmen with food and shelter. Concerning this issue, Click (2001) remarks that:

> Even a cursory overview of contraband camps suggests that life in most of the camps was very unsettled, and dependence of government support was not unusual. Many of the residents were not able to work, and the ones who did work were not always paid fairly or regularly. Consequently, a majority of the contrabands throughout the South relied to some extent on government rations and the donations of the various freedmen's relief associations. (p. 8)

It was through the establishment of Roanoke Island, as the first contraband camp to receive official designation of colony in the state of North Carolina, that the Union attempted to reconcile the social and economic empowerment of the Southern planter with that of freedmen.

Finding the various social, political, and economic forces that influenced the development of the Roanoke Island colony is an important reflection. These factors illustrate America's first attempt to provide freedmen an opportunity to define their freedom. However, when it is contextualized as an experiment, the Roanoke colony presents two major issues in the development of Reconstruction history:

1. Christian evangelicals and other social movement organizations played a significant role as emissaries of radical republicanism and the future of civil rights for freedmen.
2. White southern landowners were equally persistent and successful at repelling the spread of radical republicanism as were Northern liberals.

The focus is on the role of religious organizations in the empowerment of African-American people. Historical accounts give proof that the missionaries genuinely cared for most of the freed people. However, the shortcomings of missionaries' approach was their assumption that teaching freedmen to adopt the habits of middle-class White Northerners was the only way to prepare them to manage their freedom (Click, 2001, p. 104).

Click (2001) is emphatic on this critical point throughout her historical account. The evangelical convictions of the missionaries made it difficult for them to implement viable strategies with long-term benefit to freedmen. It is undeniable that education was a hallmark of the evangelical Christian missionary movement. However, Rev. James believed that freed people were in need of more practical resources, land ownership, and entrepreneurship. Drawing upon the manual skills that the former slaves brought with them to the island, Rev. James encouraged basket making, shoemaking, barrel making, shingle splitting and shaving, and boat building. He noted in a letter written after the Civil War that "free labor served as training for citizenship. . . . Christians and philanthropists wished to instruct the former slaves in work habits that would lift them from subservience and helplessness into a dignified independence and citizenship" (Click, 2001, p. 61).

The federal government and Northern liberals later reached similar conclusions, given the failure of the Freedmen's Bureau. It turned out that proper management of freedmen's freedom was intertwined with their participation and benefit from the American economy to pursue their happiness. Given the aforementioned tensions at work in the Colony, its failure was almost certain. Furthermore, Click (2001) identifies the harsh weather that affected crops and White southern landowners' persistence in reclaiming land that they abandoned during the Civil War from freedmen who were granted temporary ownership rights post-war by Union troops as the root causes of the Roanoke colony's economic and social deterioration (Click, 2001, p. 191). Another similarity to other Southern states found in the Roanoke colony was the power of White privilege as a controlling sentiment governing how Southern White landowners, Northern White missionaries, Southern freedmen, and the government (military/congress) implemented Reconstruction policies. At various times Southern White landowners charged the Union leaders with violating their civil rights. The constant political and social agitation of Southern White planters and their perseverance through the military occupation was a debate that garnered significant support for ending military and congressional Reconstruction.

Southerners in Roanoke, and throughout the South, believed that the infringement of their civil rights was a direct result of Reconstruction and radical republican's efforts to achieve empowerment and self-reliance for African-American communities. Accordingly, opposing freedmen rights implied support of White privilege and citizenship.

This opposition to the social, political, and economic empowerment of the freedmen throughout the South was codified on May 9, 1865 with the Amnesty Proclamation by President Andrew Johnson:

> To the end, therefore, that the authority of the government of the United States may be restored, and that peace, order, and freedom may be established, I, Andrew Johnson, President of the United States, do proclaim and declare that I hereby grant to all persons who have, directly or indirectly, participated in the existing rebellion, except as hereinafter excepted, amnesty and pardon, with restoration of all rights of property, except as to slaves, and except in cases where legal proceedings, under the laws of the United States providing for the confiscation of property of persons engaged in rebellion, have been instituted; but upon the condition, nevertheless, that every such person shall take and subscribe the following oath, (or affirmation,) and thenceforward keep and maintain said oath inviolate; and which oath shall be registered for permanent preservation... (Bergeron, 1989, pp. 128–131)

This proclamation restored land rights to Southern planters and affirmed loyalists. Ultimately, it impeded and eventually reversed the new political, social, and economic empowerment enjoyed by freedmen. In the South, land was essential to acquire wealth and securing this right to ownership was a major victory for White southerners.

A letter written in October 1866 to Maj. Gen. O. O. Howard by Samuel N. Midgett illustrates many White Southern planters' petition for the restoration of their land following the issuance of the Amnesty Proclamation. Midgett observes:

> My land was taken for the benefit of freedmen when they sought Roanoke Island as a place of refuge; was laid off into acre lots, streets opened, and cutting the timber, they built several houses, which they continue to occupy till lately in large numbers. There are now several families residing upon this land, the heads of which families could produce work at almost any place other than this Island, thereby being enabled to make a good living... I respectfully ask that my land be restored to me.... (October 20, 1866, Letters Received, RG 105, ser. 2452, NA, M843, reel 9).

The above request is further amplified when considering the increased fervor of White southerners to repel Reconstruction efforts after the assassination of President Lincoln. The Johnson presidency was marred in political tug-of-wars, which arose from democratic and conservative opposition. Ultimately, the resiliency of Southern White landowners proved stronger than the commitment of Northern Whites to their social experiment. This mini-narrative concludes with the end of Union occupation, the fading of radical republican support, the retreat of evangelicals, in this case the AMA, the rise of White Southern violence towards freedmen, and the eventual return of Roanoke Island to White landowners (Click, 2001, pp. 196, 203).

The Failure of Self-Reconstruction, 1865–1867

Some historians have argued that the main reason for the failure of Reconstruction in the South was Southern White communities' resistance to change. This prevailing historical perspective calls for further analysis. Southern White communities' racist sentiments can easily be blamed for the failure of every civil right initiative of the period. However, as argued in the previous mini-narratives, we must consider the specific context and content surrounding Reconstruction between 1865 and 1867.

Dan T. Carter (1985) believes that White Southern confederates, after the Civil War, experienced many political, social, and ideological difficulties, as they attempted to lead their own recovery and social improvement. These attempts comprise a period during Reconstruction history that Carter (1985) defines as self-Reconstruction. Carter (1985) asserts that after a careful examination of the critical months after Appomattox, when the Confederates surrendered, the assumptions of recent historians that post-war elites formed an ideologically cohesive planter class adamantly keen on resisting any change in their society is questionable. In Carter's (1985) mind, when emancipation is viewed in a broad comparative framework, White Southerners, in the absence of slavery, lacked a cohesive ideology and self-identity similar to 19th century rural land elites in other societies (p. 4).

The basis of this position is found in the following key facts that provide justification for Carter's standpoint: (a) During the Post-Civil War period, there emerged a Southern leadership that supported many of the Northern political ideals; (b) Southern notions of race led to a blind reactionary approach to self-Reconstruction; and (c) despite their grudging disobedience, the South was transformed into a free society (Carter, 1985, pp. 2–3). E. G. Richards summarizes Southern communities' sentiment at the time in his letter to Alabama's Provisional Governor Lewis Parsons, by noting that a failure to enact measures to regulate and control the behavior of the freedmen would lead to the inevitable collapse of the Southern economy (E. G. Richards to Lewis Parsons, July 21, 1865, in Alabama Governors' Papers, AA; Charleston *Daily Courier*, October 11, 1865; Jackson *Clarion*, October 11, November 12, 1865).

Considering this lack of cohesiveness and inability of the Southern White planter class to effectively organize to resist Reconstruction, Carter

(1985) further identifies two significant conditions that emerged from the failure of self-Reconstruction: (a) Post-Civil War politics and the economic development of the New South, and (b) the development of a culture of mistrust between Southern and Northern White communities. The first point is in accord with the ease of post-war Southern leaders in appropriating the slogans and rhetoric of New South economic development, despite carefully weighing their own political gains and losses, amounted to a dress rehearsal for the New South Movement of the 1870s (Carter, 1985, p. 146). While it is important to emphasize the disdain of Southern planters for what is perceived as a Northern Republican political invasion during Johnson's presidency, it is important to distinguish it from Southern political appeasement, as a process of self-empowerment.

It is undeniable that the majority of Southerners harbored racial grudges. However, their view was politically and economically informed, as the war emphasized their inability to create and manage their own political, social, and economic development. Another major concern of Southern White communities was their inability to reconstruct a social framework, post-emancipation, that could deliver similar social, political, and economic outcomes as pre-Civil War. Economic infrastructure was the main concern in the realization of White Southerners' conception of a New South. The shift in White Southerners' consciousness was quite different from that envisioned by White Northerners. They had assumed that notions of free labor would sweep aside the detritus of the proslavery argument or that the Southern White communities would defer to their Northern occupiers in matters of race relations (Carter, 1985, p. 226).

The point of contention was how to construct a society that is conducive to their economic success. Various political leaders articulated a new vision in the South that opposed secessionism. Though, these visions reinforced the social context, which was suitable to White Southerners and led to the creation of the Black Codes as a series of state restrictions on the civil rights of freedmen. Nevertheless, the New South Movement was focused on economic infrastructure, which required a change in customary practices.

The content and context of Reconstruction between 1865 and 1867 are the various implications of the Civil War and events that follow in the Summer and Fall of 1865, 1866, and 1867. These various implications and events gave rise to mistrust that widened the divide between Southern and Northern Whites (Republicans and Whigs/Unionists and Confederates). Carter's (1985) accurate narrative provides a dramatic reinterpretation of self-Reconstruction. By introducing the problem of race, Carter emphasizes that Northern political and social sentiments never fully considered how the South's economy was dependent upon slavery.

Unionist policies and political agendas, specifically, their handling of race relations always impinged upon the economic viability of the planter class. Southern economy couldn't thrive without slavery. The Unionists' position was unequivocal and demanded a transition to a free labor economy, in which Black labor could be contracted and converted into Black empowerment. Also, the conservatives' standpoint was also clear in claiming that freedmen did not deserve the right to participate in southern economy, as independent producers. This debate would develop differently in various Southern states, tilting towards either side at various times. However, as previously mentioned, Northerners seemed to consistently underestimate the persistence of Southerners to repel Reconstruction efforts, while Southerners remained committed to developing a social, political, and economic system based on pre-Civil War ideologies and principles.

The Union League, Freedmen's Bureau, and Reconstruction

This mini-narrative will assess the work of two authors, Michael Fitzgerald (1989) and Paul A. Cimbala (1997) to ascertain the level of political activism and self-reconstruction that freedmen achieved through their membership in social organizations and association with the Freedmen's Bureau.

Fitzgerald (1989) thinks that the Union (Loyal) League (League) insurgency is one of the largest African American social movements in American history and critiques its relative historical neglect. He argues that the Union League's proselytizing helped plant Republicanism among freedmen and the League became one of the Ku Klux Klan's major targets, which is proof of its significance and effectiveness (p. 4). From Du Bois to Downing, historians have downplayed the social significance of the politicization of freedmen through the League. The abandonment of gang labor and the politicization of the freedmen with congressional Reconstruction took a toll on the cotton-based economy of the South. This struggle over Black labor placed freedmen and their League at the center of post-emancipation agricultural society. Through the League, they struggled to increase their autonomy and fulfill the promise of participation in the United States as citizens.

The League benefited freedmen in that it provided (a) essential political education to assume civil rights, and (b) a long-lasting commitment to political activism and the value of enfranchisement for social mobility. As freedmen learned more about politics and became more skeptical about their allies, they grew more aggressive. African-American communities began forwarding more radical demands and promoting their own leaders (Fitzgerald, 1989, p. 71). One of the early lessons of Reconstruction for freedmen was that their social, political, and economic gains could be repealed anytime. Thus, their continued political activity was always geared toward the non-reversal of their new social status. However, as they grew wiser they also developed a more radical approach to ensuring their own autonomy. Freedmen wanted their own land, businesses, social institutions, political organizations, and control of their own destiny, while actively pursuing their civil rights. Fitzgerald (1989) reinforces this fact in the following statement:

> A conservative black, describing the situation in Alabama in the late 1880s reported that freedmen saw the Republicans as their salvation, still fearing they would be put back into slavery, or something of that sort... [Y]ou might as well talk about killing them, as about them not voting the Republican ticket. Clearly, Southern Blacks had not forgotten the struggle for Radical ideals. (p. 239)

Furthermore, Fitzgerald (1989) found that freedmen were actively engaged in group-based (community-oriented) political activism to demand the protection of their civil rights and they sought the complete realization of the political promises made by the Republican party. The Union League through its radicalism fed the freedmen's desire to find a vehicle that would give voice to their concerns and most importantly a platform on which to express their views.

In addition, the League provided an invisible, yet critical social network for freedmen through its secret practices. This fed the freedmen's sense of purpose, strength, and connectedness to something more than themselves; namely, fraternity. Lastly, the League reinforced the convictions of freedmen to never accept slavery or any social, political, or economic system that is akin to slavery. Their membership in the League strengthened their conviction to reject Southern planter society's practices such as: sharecropping, tenant farming, Black codes, women working, and other cultural realties that reminded them of their slave days.

The League instilled in the minds of freedmen that Reconstruction was a meaningful progress and could result in their full-citizenship in the United States. James Lusk Alcorn, a reporter, in 1865 wrote in his report on the political situation in Mississippi that

> once convinced they could speak their minds, freedmen needed little urging to denounce the memory of slavery and those who continued to oppress them. In the words of one rank and file Leaguer, freedmen talked pretty

big' at meetings, and they took pride in rejecting even the symbols of white supremacy. The League's organizing technique encouraged a militant approach to political issues, and this tendency became more pronounced over time. (James Lusk Alcorn, views of the Honorable J. L. Alcorn on the Political Situation of Mississippi [N.p., 1867], 3; KKK Report, IX, 685)

Also, Cimbala (1997) argues that an analysis of the Georgia Freedmen's Bureau (Bureau) sheds light on Reconstruction failed to facilitate lasting change in the United States. He suggests that understanding Reconstruction requires understanding the Bureau (p. xx). The Freedmen's Bureau grappled with many challenges in Georgia as it sought to implement government policies and reintegrate ex-slaves into the cultural fabric of Georgian society. Unique to this work is the contiguity between the quadric-tenuous aims of the Georgia Bureau to (a) stay in tune with the most modern political ideology of Washington; (b) minimize and suppress white Georgian's acts of resistance, while changing their perception of the Bureau; (c) solicit and sustain philanthropic assistance of Northerners; and (d) assist and prepare freed people for life post-Bureau.

These four aims provide a context by which to assess the effectiveness of Bureau goals in assisting freedmen with their integration into southern U.S. culture. Using the Bureau as a context for understanding Reconstruction post 1867, Cimbala (1997) provides insight into the political, social and economic, internal, and external struggles of the Freedmen's Bureau in Georgia as it strove to negotiate the expectations of ex-slaves (freedman), ex-rebels (White Georgians), Northerners (Yankees), and the government (in Washington and Bureau). The educational legacy of the Bureau and efforts of the Bureau to integrate freedmen into the community are particularly interesting.

Even as the Bureau began to terminate its other major Reconstruction activities, its men continued to encourage the freed people's educational efforts with a vigor that seemed to suggest they wished to leave behind some kind of legacy (Cimbala, 1997, p. 108). The Bureau found it difficult to maintain any initiative or program that would provide long lasting assistance to freed people. Furthermore, despite having significant temporary impact on the social (mediating conflicts), political (encouraging voting), and economic (providing avenues for land ownership) life of freed people, none would survive the attacks of White Southern anti-Black sentiments. Given that the Bureau was continuously strapped for resources and lacked political and militaristic support, it had to adopt promoting education as its core motif.

Each previous mini-narrative echoes the inability of local leaders, representing the state or the nation, particularly Bureau agents, to repel White Southern planters' acts of resistance. These acts of resistance have been well documented. As mentioned previously by Fitzgerald (1989) the rise of the Ku Klux Klan (KKK) was a significant strategy of White Southerners to impede Reconstruction. However, Bureau representatives intervened more frequently in situations where planters abused freedmen workers' rights on tenant farms by overcharging for services, adding additional costs, and violating other terms of contracts. By advocating something as basic to Northern goals as simple justice in labor relations, Bureau agents put their lives on the line for the freed people and for Reconstruction, for which they attracted violence from White Georgians (Cimbala, 1997, pp. 72–73).

The KKK still effectively intimidated freedmen and Northern Whites by lynchings, fire bombings, and harassment, especially of teachers, as KKK members and supporters had a disdain for Black education. This fact is reflected in the vision of the Georgia Bureau's education superintendent, which is articulated by Gilbert Eberhart. In the Spring of 1866, he argued that Yankee teachers should not invite trouble by kissing Black babies, proclaiming belief in Black equality, or replying in kind to White insults on the streets of Augusta, Georgia. He also urged the teachers to be prudent, which is a wise advice given the already hostile environment in which they worked and the limited resources available to the Bureau for policing White violence (Cimbala, 1997, pp. 126–127). In either case, one of the Bureau's greatest flaws was also its greatest strength; namely, their commitment to the future of freed people to exist autonomously from their White counterparts.

Unionists and Scalawags

This mini-narrative follows a similar historical trajectory as the previous one. It assesses the importance of freedmen's political activism during Reconstruction. In her account of political activism during Reconstruction, Margaret M. Storey (2004) argues that the experiences of loyalists during wartime and Reconstruction offer an exceptional opportunity to address a range of issues that are critical to the study of the South and the Civil War. These issues include analyses of the social and political factors that affect loyalty between White Southerners and freedmen to the Union.

By focusing on the loyalty of Unionist in Alabama, Storey (2004) assesses how these men (White yeomen and freed Black individuals) expressed their commitment to the United States and the Republican party despite being a political minority within the Confederacy. She observes that Alabamians, who were loyal Unionists, believed in their country, social and political values, honor, and pride with a similar dedication as Southern confederates. Southern White Union loyalists shared many of the same nationalistic and federalist ideologies as their Confederate neighbors. However, she finds it peculiar that White Southern Unionists' commitment to develop a culture of resistance, in spite of being ostracized by their Southern comrades, to secession. At the heart of this mini-narrative is the willingness of Southern White Union loyalists to live as outsiders and refusing to abandon their Southern homes, while also refusing to abandon their Republican values.

Similar to the internal conflicts faced by freedmen, Storey (2004) offers the following two points for consideration:

1. For many Southern White liberals their commitment to the Union outweighed the inherent threats of the political climate and culture.
2. As a result of the constant political instability, White Southerners developed a deeper animosity against confederates (scalawags) than freedmen.

Storey (2004) writes:

> The political culture that gave rise to unionism in the Confederacy was a southern political culture—it was premised on hierarchical and reciprocal kinship and neighborhood relationships, and it was often refracted through the prism of slavery and the values and challenges of a slave society. (p. 55)

This is a major fact. White Southern loyalists in Alabama were constantly threatened with injury to their person, property, or loved ones. Their families were ostracized and they were forced to create alternative social relationships. Through their unfailing commitment to the Union, these social relationships evolved into a political consciousness and radical involvement in the war through espionage and enlistment. The role of the freedman cannot be excluded from this discussion, as most times these yeomen displayed similar coercive acts against the Confederacy. Either way, it remains clear that loyalists were Southerners who are primarily lovers of their culture and their way of life, despite color or consciousness.

The participation of Alabamians in guerilla warfare is an essential point of Storey's thesis. Their willingness to support the Union despite major impediments defines their loyalty. Additionally, these loyalists formed the base of unionism, as a movement in the South. The experience of guerilla warfare during the last years of the war itself, stemming from several years of intimidation, abuse, and exile, compelled Unionists to commit to stringent solutions to the problem of treason against the Union. This thirst for justice and retribution, however, would result in a most bitter legacy (Storey, 2004, p. 169).

Differentiated not by slaveholding status, quality of farmland, or wealth, loyalty becomes the single distinguishing characteristic between Unionists and Scalawags. Loyalty was the key distinguishing characteristic between Unionists and Scalawags independently of their slaveholding status, the quality of their farmland, and wealth. Unionists' loyalty is an outcome of their politicization of cultural practices and values. Unionists in Alabama defended their home, as a strategy to define what it meant to be American. There were no possibilities of political reconciliation for those who were deemed as traitors. They were neighbors with extreme differences. Storey's (2004) account of Unionists in Alabama provides a new dynamic in Reconstruction history that blurs the lines of race, hatred, and nationality through an emphasis on loyalty.

Community Perspectives

William McKee Evans (1995) provides an interesting historical reflection on the complexity of life in the conservative South, post-Civil War, during presidential, military, and radical Reconstruction. Evans (1995) recasts the crisis of Cape Fear, North Carolina. By combining primary source materials, personal narratives, and historical accounts, he provides a general perspective on community life in the South. Through this mini-narrative, North Carolina, like much of the confederate South, was unique in its dealing with the issues of freedmen, Republican politics, and economics in a post-Civil War society while being steadfast in its desire to maintain its particular social order.

Evans (1995) states that through his analysis, North Carolinians coped with various crises during Reconstruction, revealing how they navigated the new political, social, and economic mazes, using blueprints from their past (p. xviii). There are two key points worthy of reflection:

1. Increased political engagement led to increased conflicts between Black republicans and White conservatives.
2. As Southern politics began to become increasingly polarized along economic and racial lines, businessmen and time merchants became influential local political leaders and power brokers.

Realizing the extent of their newly acquired freedom, and sensing the reluctance of Southern conservatives to affirm their rights to full citizenship in the state and Union, these freedmen chose to use their power of suffrage, as a primary vehicle for self-empowerment.

Evans (1995) explains how through the ratification campaign, White conservatives based their strategy on the image of a superstitious Negro who would flee in terror at the sight of a white sheet (p. 101). In fact, the political conflict emerging between Black republicans and White conservatives in North Carolina was an outcome of Black empowerment. Participating in various electioneering activities, and party-based politics, African-American communities in North Carolina publically displayed their dissatisfaction with local and state politics. However, their political agitation was met with fierce reactions aimed at repressing their attempts at social mobility and civic engagement through the intimidations and terrorist acts of the KKK and the Lagrange Gang.

Freedmen in North Carolina and across the South experienced unprecedented political success, as a result of the increase in their political engagement. A Black newspaper of the time, *The Loyal Georgian*, reported morosely that

> the future looks dark, and we predict, that we are entering upon the greatest political contest that has ever agitated the people of the country-a contest, in which, we of the South must be for the most part spectators; not indifferent spectators, for it is about us that the political battle is fought. The issue is fairly joined. (Georgia Republican Party, *The Loyal Georgian*, March 3, 1866)

The political engagement of African-American communities posed a major social threat to the conservative White residents of Cape Valley. Full citizenship for African Americans and their political involvement were perceived as major threats by those residents for whom maintaining the social order and politics of the pre-war South a necessity.

Given that the centrality of freedmen to the Reconstruction history in the United States is more evident considering its historical mini-narrative, the critical question is then: "How can Black empowerment be synonymous with White oppression?" Evans' (1995) historical account of Reconstruction emphasizes this negative correlation in his account of the struggle to repress Black republicanism as the major communal conflict of Reconstruction.

A conservative South suspended somewhere between slavery and democracy, was tailored made to suit the taste of the powerful and growing class of time merchants (Evan, 1995, p. 253). This perspective reflects the emerging power of the merchant classes in Cape Valley, which results from the economic changes experienced post-war and during Reconstruction. Evans links the end of the war and the emancipation of slaves, or at least the new social position of freedmen, with the need for North Carolinians to develop a new market economy. Railroads, mills, lumber, and time merchants replaced many of the agricultural based pre-war Southern economic systems in North Carolina. As such, these men, often in second professions, through their wealth, became targets of political parties.

The merchant social class was at the center of the rise (or return) of the Conservative party to North Carolina, particularly Cape Valley. The economic success of the South was thought to be in direct opposition to the education and political uplift of freedmen. The silent shift in the political landscape of the South may be easily overlooked in this mini narrative. Conservatives were beginning to increase in congressional representation, just as Republican sentiment in the North was weakening. Southerners were seeking stability and the increased politicization of freedmen posed a social inhibitor. The period from July 26, 1868 to August 4, 1870, the date when the Conservatives regained control of the legislature, was in certain respects the crest of radical Reconstruction (Evans, 1995, p. 251). Notwithstanding, the U.S. political and social economies were very much dependent on a political and socially stable South. The planter and merchant classes' opposition to the enfranchisement of African-American communities affected the country negatively. Unfortunately, the Union leadership could not risk the loss or further deterioration of the South as a viable exporter of American goods and a center of trade and commerce in the United States.

Comparative Perspectives

The narrative history of political, social, and economic debate in 19th century United States provides the historical context for Reconstruction and the continued debate over the role of black labor in a post-emancipation era is at its center. Foner (1983) elaborates upon this context by integrating the significant aspects of the previous Reconstruction mini-narratives into a process by which economic and political structures inform our understanding of race relations post-slavery.

As an approach to historiography, close reading of Foner's (1983) work allows us to consider Reconstruction as a struggle between former masters and slaves (p. 5). Du Bois (1929) provides the context for such critical assessment in the statement below:

> What the Negro did was to wait, look and listen, and try to see where his interest lay. There was no use in seeking refuge in an army which was not an

army of freedom; and there was no sense in revolting against armed masters who were conquering the world. As soon, however, as it became clear that the Union armies would not or could not return fugitive slaves, and that the masters with all their fume and fury were uncertain of victory, the slave entered upon a general strike against slavery by the same methods that he had used during the period of the fugitive slave. He ran away to the first place of safety and offered his services to the Federal Army. So that in this way it was really true that he served his former master and served the emancipating army; and it was also true that this withdrawal and bestowal of his labor decided the war. (p. 57)

Foner (1983) assumed that the experiences of freedmen in the Caribbean, Brazil, and the United States were similar. Foner takes it for granted that their experiences of emancipation are shaped by their struggles to change oppressive political and economic systems. Foner (1983) provides two perspectives to support his standpoint:

1. Reconstruction in the South centered on a struggle over the control of resources and relationships.
2. To fully understand Reconstruction, one must understand the international legacy of emancipation.

The priority of former masters was to maintain social superiority that they acquired through slavery. Everywhere, emancipation was succeeded by struggle for control of the scarce resources of plantation economies, paramount among them—the labor of the former slaves themselves (Foner, 1983, p. 37). On the other hand, emancipation inspired an entrepreneurial ambition amongst freedmen, as a means of social uplift and independence from the authority of their former masters. Both former masters and freedmen failed to acknowledge that the collapse of the plantation system was unavoidable and the need to reinvent their social roles in a new political economic era.

Foner (1983) explains that the unresolved legacy of emancipation remains part of our racial institutions, attitudes, and the social dislocations around us and the world, more than a century after the demise of slavery (p. 110). Accordingly, Reconstruction can be considered as part of a post-emancipation era, rather than a post-Civil War history. Following in the historical footsteps of Du Bois (1929), the significance of Reconstruction lies in the development of a new sociopolitical structure and constitutional legacy, which was established to ensure that freedmen are allowed to exercise their rights and practice their citizenship. The mini-narratives that follow will focus on the life of Black freedom; specifically, the commerce of freedom and how it is transacted politically, socially, and economically. The main issue is how the reconstitution of the Union benefitted from Reconstruction. The key concern is the protection of freedmen civil rights during the constitutional Reconstruction period.

Black Labor

In order to contextualize the discussion of the role of Black labor and its evolution into a struggle for Black freedom, we rely on the work of Sharon Holt (2000). Holt argues that North Carolina freedmen relied on their social and personal perseverance and determination to deal with the complexity of life after slavery. Holt takes it for granted that acts of self-empowerment were at the center of the evolution of Black freedom. Freed people's efforts won them the right to work, save, build, and define themselves and their communities on their own terms (p. xxiii). The freedom of African-American communities is dependent upon their power. A plausible take on Reconstruction is that it lingers throughout U.S. history, despite the threat of dissipation. However, close scrutiny reveals two central motifs in the legacy of Reconstruction:

1. African-American communities' freedom often reflected White supremacy.
2. The use of Black labor to develop Black institutions allowed freedmen to take ownership of their civil rights in an unprecedented fashion.

Holt (2000) thinks that employers tried to overcome freed people's resistance with both, violence and stratagem, not only because employers wanted their labor, but because freed people valued the control of women and children's work time as an emblem of freedom (pp. 35, 43). Throughout Reconstruction, the Southern planter class were often perplexed by the tenacity of a people they perceived as inferior. Holt sheds light on the desire of Black men to be free from their masters and control their own lands. However, Black men perpetuated similar strategies of domination on tenant farms, which is illustrated in their treatment of women. Furthermore, Holt views this practice of domination as a desire to protect their women from intense labor in the plantations. It also shows Freedmen's major obstacle in a post-slavery economy, namely how to overcome their own use of former masters' strategies of control against each other.

Holt (2000) draws out an implication of Reconstruction that will have to be addressed in each subsequent historical time period by freedmen: to create an appropriate self concept and identity during post-emancipation.

It is a major fact that freed people invested considerable political capital, economic leverage, and endured personal injuries to secure the right to labor on their own behalf. With that power, they worked every possibility of the Southern social system, and every opening in the Southern economy to bring emancipation the resources to create freedom (Holt, 2000, p. 23). Ultimately, freedmen exercised their freedoms from a socially inferior perspective: The myriad shortcomings and accomplishments of Reconstruction, particularly in North Carolina, are proof that it was an experiment in the formation of Black consciousness. Black consciousness means the self-perception and identity that African-American communities acquired from their social, political, and economic experiences as freed people.

The emergence of Black consciousness is one of the greatest results of the struggle for civil and labor rights for freedmen. The process of creating Black schools and churches echoed, in its particularity, the general outlines of how Blacks and Whites adjusted to emancipation (Holt, 2000, p. 102). African-American communities in North Carolina in comparison to those throughout the United States were very aggressive in their need to establish churches and schools. These activities are illustrated in the missionary work of the African Methodist Episcopal Church (AME) led by Bishop Daniel Alexander Payne and Pastor William H. Heard; the African Methodist Episcopal Zion Church (AMEZ) led by Bishop William Hillery; the AMA led by James Lowery, a Black Wilmington carpenter turned teacher and member of the Baptist Church; and the Presbyterian Church through their Board of Elections.

Religious organizations, particularly Black churches, as Carter G. Woodson argued, were the most important institutions in African-American communities because they fulfilled the needs for political, educational, and moral reform (Holt, 2000, p. 128). As cornerstones for building a strong society, African Americans, with the assistance of northern Whites, worked independently to use education and God to encourage political participation, social integration, economic mobility, leadership development, and most importantly to espouse African American social values and norms.

The Role of Violence in Reconstruction

During post-Civil War, power dwelled in the political party. The most powerful party controlled the destiny of the state and to what extent Reconstruction processes prevailed. This fact was most blatant in Tennessee. This mini-narrative provides a historical account of Southern Whites' response to the possible rise in African-American political, social, and economic power. Ben

H. Severance (2005) provides his historical account of Reconstruction on the premise that the militiamen who served in the State Guard were both radical leaders and followers who had a vested interest in ensuring that the Radical party assumed political power and legitimacy throughout the state. His argument is that the Tennessee State Guard was remarkably effective at enforcing the Reconstruction policies of the Radical Republican government (p. xvii). Moreover, Severance makes two important points:

1. Anti-radical movements prevented the full implementation of Reconstruction.
2. Anti-radical movements are fueled when African Americans are viewed as the primary defenders of their civil rights.

One major impact of the Civil War in Tennessee, as witnessed throughout the South, was the animosity between Confederates and Unionists. Severance (2005) points out that after the surrender of the Confederacy and subsequent end of the Civil War, Tennessee's dilemma was how to restore civil order. In Tennessee, loyalists, unionists, and the majority of the latter refused to support emancipation. The issue in Tennessee was to decide which group would have political power. Should power rest with the Unionists, who were considered radical social reformers? Or the Loyalists, who were considered social conservatives?

Ultimately, the fear of racial equality and civil rights for freedmen became associated with the Unionists and the basis of the anti-radical movement. It was this movement, and particularly its use of violence, that prevented the full implementation of Congress Reconstruction agenda. Tennessee was unique in population, geography, and commitment of Loyalists and Unionists to use force to support their political agendas. Loyalists led riots, planned assassinations, organized political protests, and did anything in their power to confuse and complicate the Union's plans to treat Tennessee as other Southern states.

Throughout Tennessee, and other states in the South, violence emerged as a means to curb and encourage Black communities' involvement in politics, and society violence was used as a loyalist tactic to stymie Unionist political activism: recruitment, electioneering, campaigning, organizing, and so forth. Concomitantly, Unionists viewed military force, as a strategy employed by Republicans to maintain civil order. However, the role of Black men in the militias is one of the great lessons of Reconstruction to have come from Tennessee. While Black labor was needed, the protection of Black labor was a unique approach applied by Unionists.

During his election of 1867, Governor Brownlow tried to recruit, enlist, and engage the Black population by empowering them socially as military men. Severance (2005) argues that by using the State Guard to help win the election of 1867, the Brownlow administration learned two valuable lessons:

1. Black militia units were at least as much a liability as an asset.
2. Reconstruction in parts of the state, especially in West Tennessee, was going to require the continued use of military force (p. 143).

It is mind-boggling that the reinforcement of Black empowerment during Reconstruction required the involvement of local and state militia throughout the South. However, this single act contributed to the fears of conservatives and anti-radicals and was stopped.

As previously stated, Tennessee was peculiar for the use of force in settling disagreements and the governor learned that once military force is used, it would be difficult to prevent further acts of violence, given that both parties used violence to express their discontent. Despite these negative outcomes, local and state principalities began to abhor election season and anticipated its occurrence with increased armament. As time unfolds, fraternal orders of police and national guards planned their activities around elections. It was a common belief that the safety of a Southern town or city was connected to Black disenfranchisement. Accordingly, it became prevalent that to keep the peace freedmen should discontinue their political activism.

The North, Religion, and Reconstruction

The previous mini-narratives tell the story of the weakening of Northern Republican liberal sentiment in light of increased violence and the government's unwillingness to provide adequate resources to support a military Reconstruction. Edward J. Blum (2005) writes from the premise that the religious idealism and radicalism of the American nation provided the impetus for Northern and Southern White reconciliation. Blum (2005) offers insight into how the religious fervor of the late 19th century provided America with an acceptable mainstream alternative, which is to transition from a social justice ideology focused on the empowerment of the freedmen towards a social reconstructivism focused on fostering racial harmony amongst Whites.

From politicians to preachers and merchants to farmers, White Northerners and Southerners began to couch their post-Civil War hopes in a theological socialism that later transformed into Protestant Christianity, which served as a civic religion. Blum (2005) makes the most crucial assessment of the end of Reconstruction, by observing that "forgetting and abandoning commitments to racial justice were essential to the remaking of the White republic" (p. 15). This new ideal was intended to define Reconstruction by identifying a triangular arrangement between Yankees, Confederates, and African Americans. Religion played a crucial role in shaping the social and political identity of White and Black America.

From the mid 1860s to the 1870s, a diverse crowd of Northern Whites used religious narratives, ideas, and metaphors to justify sectional reconciliation and racial discrimination in a variety of popular media (Blum, 2005, p. 118). Once again, the use of religion by Northern Whites was apparent in the evangelization activities of the AMA in the South. Reverend Patton, an AMA spokesperson raising funds in Scotland attempted to ease White concern for the enfranchisement of freedmen with the following statement: "Their vote could be controlled only by bringing in as a counterpoise four million of negroes-Protestant Negroes every man of them. The blacks thereby would be the salvation of our country" (The Freedmen of America, Report of Public Meeting in the Free Assembly Hall, Edinburgh, July 2, 1866 Edinburgh, Scotland: Wm. Cruikshank [1866]), p. 9, reporting an address by AMA agent Reverend Patton).

The AMA was clear in its rhetoric to assure Whites in the United States and abroad that the emancipation and ultimate empowerment of the freedmen would strengthen their cause without changing the socially inferior status of Blacks. The history of the role of religion in the birth of a new nation post-Civil War begins after the death of Lincoln with continued opposition of Southern Whites to military and presidential Reconstruction. This steadfast opposition led to the need for increased religious fervor. The Great Awakening movement was conducive to the evangelization of the South, which led to a call by many White religious leaders for reconciliation. The premise was that divine influences were leading the nation towards expansion into the West, illustrated in the war of 1898 and any internal strife, such as debates over the status of African-Americans would inhibit the forecasted growth of the United States. White Protestant Northerners cloaked their message in religious language and influence to reach out to their Southern brothers and sisters, and some freedmen, to assist the country. While the evangelistic activities of the White Northern Church increased, W. E. B. Du Bois, and other African-American leaders, urged the nation not to conciliate blindly and abandon the racial justice agenda and hope of the Republican party. Dubois (1970) made the following comment: "There was one thing that the white South feared more than Negro dishonesty, ignorance, and incompetency, and that was Negro honesty, knowledge, and efficiency" (p. 130).

The fear of the role of African Americans in society versus a need for White America to forge a new direction in its history was the basis for the rise of religious zeal in the collective imagination and the need for experiencing citizenship during Reconstruction. It is thus undeniable that religion played an important role in the failure of Reconstruction. Other historians agree that the evangelization of freed people during Reconstruction also had a crippling effect of the White South as well. The historian Claude G. Bowers (1929) writes:

> The years of Reconstruction were years of revolutionary turmoil, with the elemental passions predominant. The prevailing note was one of tragedy.... Never have American public men in responsible positions, directing the destiny of the nation, been so brutal, hypocritical, and corrupt. The constitution was treated as a doormat on which politicians and army officers wiped their feet after wading in the muck.... The Southern people literally were put to the torture... [by] rugged conspirators... [who] assumed the pose of philanthropists and patriots. (p. v)

Through evangelical Protestantism, defined as the supremacy of Whiteness, the supremacy of the United States and the supremacy of Christ had again become viewed as one in the same (Blum, 2005, p. 249). Blum (2005) ends his critique of previous historical accounts of Reconstruction and the time period (late 19th century) by identifying the melding of three ideals; namely, culture, politics, and religion into a national identity. These ideals were illustrated by the withdrawal of federal troops and the end of Reconstruction.

Close attention to the evolution of Black empowerment throughout Reconstruction history, specifically the period of religious fervor reveals the reemergence of White privilege veiled in Christian ideology. The theology of the cross was the instrument through which rights for freedmen were conceptualized as obstacles to national healing. More important than the ability of Christian theology to support Black civil rights, it was used to promulgate a gospel of reconciliation between the divided Union and Confederacy. Unfortunately, there was not enough room on the cross to crucify slavery, racism, secession, and the demons of Civil War politics.

The Constitutional Legacy

Charting the historical narrative of the development of Reconstruction in the United States requires an understanding of the ideological basis and intent of Reconstruction. This understanding is achievable through a consideration of the constitutional legacy of Reconstruction. The constitutional legacy of Reconstruction articulates the various intents, which define the spirit of Reconstruction. It articulates the intent of politicians, who wrote, argued, and shaped constitutional amendments and other legislation; the intent of lawyers who petitioned and argued cases in defense of Reconstruction ideals; the intent of judges who decided the role of the federal government in ensuring the protection of freedmen's civil rights. This history is narrated by two authors, Howard N. Meyer (1973) and Robert M. Goldman (2007).

Meyer (1973) reflects on the political and social legacies of the 14th Amendment, which extend the Bill of Rights protections to freedmen. He contextualizes his historical account of the 14th Amendment in a lack of political understanding of the U.S. Constitution (as written in 1787) and the impetus of the founding fathers, specifically the role of the federal government in relation to the states when considering the protection of civil rights. The first American Constitution, with its Bill of Rights, created a framework for the founding fathers to consolidate their gains during the American Revolution and the need to protect the individual from a tyrannical group.

Meyer (1973) argues that the spirit of the first Constitution was so radically amended with the ratification of the 13th, 14th, and 15th amendments that there was created a second American Constitution, with the purpose to expand the protection of civil rights by the federal government to former slaves. Meyer focused on the impacts of the 14th Amendment and considers it the Big Fourteen by marking its congressional birth in 1868, its judicial death with the beginning of the Slaughter House case in 1873, and its subsequent rebirth through the U.S. Supreme Court cases *Gitlow v. New York* in 1925 and *Brown v. Bd. of Education of Topeka*, Kansas in 1954. As such, Meyer (1973) argues that the Constitution of the United States is founded upon a perceived betrayal of the framers' commitment to protecting the rights of all its citizens (p. xi).

Goldman (2007) compares and contrasts the impact of two cases brought before the U.S. Supreme Court: *U.S. v. Reese* and *U.S. v. Cruikshank*. The premise of these cases is the judicial branch of the government's interpretation of the application of the 15th (Reese decision) and the 14th (Cruikshank decision) Amendments. Goldman (2007) concludes that these two cases illustrated both ends of a continuum that characterized White Southerners' response to the above amendment and Congress's intent to enforce these laws (pp. 5–8). Goldman (2001) provides insight into how these cases shaped the political reality of the time period and conducts an analysis of their lasting effects on 20th and 21st century civil rights activism.

Conclusion

The Significance of Black Higher Education in the Reconstruction Era

The history of Black education in the United States is inseparable with its development into a nation and ultimate world power. Particularly, the development of Black higher education cannot be contemplated independently of Reconstruction history. This discourse sheds a peculiar light on critical issues that permeate the history of Reconstruction: post-Civil War reunification of the North (Union) and South (Confederacy), endurance of federalist ideology (one nation under God politics), protection of the natural and civil rights of Southern loyalists and former confederates, protection of the natural and civil rights of former slaves and their descendants, transition from an agricultural to an industrial economy, role of the federal government in protecting the natural and civil rights of citizens, protection of states' rights, and the struggle of African Americans for Civil Rights.

The relationship between Black higher education and the rise of the United States as a nation leads A. J. M. Milne (1968) to write:

> There are then two ways in which a society's economy affects its way of life. One is indirect, the greater the productivity of these activities the better the opportunities for intrinsically valuable activities. The other is direct and arises out of the fact that a society's methods of production and technology are not separate from but form an integral part of its way of life. (Milne, 1968, p. 227)

Milne's observation reinforces the view that in an industrial society, individual success in gaining access to the economic aspects of governmental freedom is measured by individual involvements in political activities (i.e., voting rights, representation, preferential legislation, economic resources, and political influence).

These exercises of freedom allow freed persons to: (a) indirectly engage in activities that actualize productivity (i.e., social relationships) through their influence, and (b) overtly engage in visible activities that show potential for increased productivity (i.e., education, profession, etc.), amassing a wealth of experience.

Belz (2000), Foner (1983), and Holt (2000) elaborate African Americans' use of self-empowerment scripts. Also, these scholars acknowledge that Du Bois (1929) offers the best lens to view the significance of Black higher education in the Reconstruction era. These scholars concur that Du Bois's view helps us grasp how a philosophical understanding of capitalist and market economies influence race relations and the empowerment of freedmen. Du Bois (1929) commented:

> Karl Marx—had not yet published Das Kapital to prove to men that economic power underlies politics. . . . They did not know that when they let the dictatorship of labor be overthrown in the South they surrendered the hope of democracy in America for all men. The espousal of the doctrine of Negro inferiority by the South was primarily because of economic motives and the inter-connected political urge necessary to support slave industry. . . . The South could say that the Negro, even when brought into modern civilization, could not be civilized, and that, therefore, he and the other colored peoples of the world were so far inferior to the whites that the white world had a right to rule mankind for their own selfish interests. (pp. 591–592)

It is safe to infer from Du Bois's observation that the success of the Reconstruction experiment would take more than emancipation and military oversight. In his mind, the United States should have committed to invest in the freed people as a new type of social capital, which is fit to contribute equally to the prosperity of the nation.

Governmental freedom in a capitalist society is measured by individual ability to increase and actualize potential through access to various social resources. Any freedom given is a governmental investment of resources with the expectation that a valuable product would be gained in return. Basically, in capitalist economies, society operates as the context for participation in the freedom of production. This was the major issue in Reconstruction Georgia, North Carolina, and Tennessee where the freedom of African-Americans amounted to being allowed to participate in production. The individuals of a given community maintain the right to invest their resources into the purchase of commodities that bring them closer to their desired goal. This quasi-agriculturalist system of harvesting (modes of production) has been defined, philosophically, as laissez-faire liberalism.

This account of modes of production views society as a field of investigation in addition to the individuals and the state, each adhering to certain laws of self-regulating competition (Skirbekk & Gilje, 2001, p. 266). In this context many Southern Whites found it difficult, post-Civil War, to recognize African-Americans as a community of stakeholders in the economy of freedom, as participants in the American experiment, or co-investors with a similar vision/goal for the future. In order to be perceived as a community requires that the individuals must share in the power of the state. Some

Southern Whites were reluctant to share state power with African Americans, which is the cause of all political, social, or economical struggles in the life of African Americans in the United States.

This history of the struggle for African-American civil rights is the second part of a movement for access to the freedoms and rights of all human beings and citizens in the United States. The history of this struggle is about African-Americans' struggle for civil rights and their efforts to transform themselves from slaves to doctors, actors, businessmen, or any other guild that enjoys full citizenship. Any theory of Black education must include the continuous promotion of African-Americans' efforts to fully participate in citizenship.

As Cimbala (1997) found in Georgia about the Freedmen's Bureau, Holt (2000) found about North Carolina, and Evans (1995) found about Cape Valley, education continues to be the single most influential institution created to aid African Americans with their transformation from slaves to citizens, more specifically Black education. The education of African Americans is such a significant historical artifact that after considering the historical mini-narratives of Reconstruction history in the United States that constitutional amendments and Black educational institutions remain active in the 21st century.

4

Founding Presidents and Their Colleges

This chapter assesses the personal and professional lives of Bishop Payne and President Joseph Robert. It focuses on their respective presidencies through chronicles of the founding of the institutions to uncover the motivations, interests, professional accomplishments, and challenges. It is particularly sensitive to the effects of their presidential legacy in the time period and the supports each president received from their respective institutions.

A Short Biography of Rt. Rev. Dr. Daniel A. Payne

The life of the Rt. Rev. Dr. Daniel Alexander Payne (Bishop Payne) begins in the hill country of Charleston, SC, where he was born on February 24, 1811, to London and Martha Payne (Payne, 1968, p. 11). Mr. London Payne was the son of two free persons from Virginia. However, Bishop Payne's father was captured then transported to the port of Charleston to be sold into slavery to a house of a sign painter (Payne, 1968, p. 12). London Payne was dedicated to attain his freedom, which he purchased at the cost of 1,000

Not For Ourselves Alone, pages 65–89
Copyright © 2019 by Information Age Publishing

dollars. Martha Payne was a descendent of a mixed marriage between a slave father and a mother from the Carolinas' Catawba Indians. She lived as a free woman throughout her life.

In his memoires, Bishop Payne recollects his childhood with great fondness. However, he regrets both his parents' death prior to his 10th birthday: His father died when he was four and his mother passed away when he was 9 years of age. Despite their short lives, his parents were able to instill in him a deep spiritual desire for God and interest in the development of his intellectual abilities. They were members of the Methodist Episcopal Church. Bishop Payne remembered vividly the prayers on the family altar and countless hours in church services when he accompanied his father, who served as a deacon in the church and his mother who served as a class leader (Payne, 1968, pp. 12–13). While his parents ignited an eternal inner flame for spirituality and knowledge, Bishop Payne credits his grandaunt, Mrs. Sarah Bordeaux, with fanning those fires in his life and encouraging him towards the cultivation of a strong sense of morality and a noble character (Payne, 1968, p. 13).

Educational Background

One of Bishop Payne's greatest gifts was his intellect which was recognized by his peers. William S. Scarborough called him the "intellectual Moses of his race" and the *Christian Recorder* compared him to Moses: "[Bishop Payne was a] leader and teacher, he did for us what no other did or could" (Gaustad, 1972, Introduction). More than anything, Bishop Payne emphasized his love and passion for education as his most treasured gift. Bishop Payne recounted that his highest aim was to be an educator (Payne, 1968, p. 45), and his educational journey served as the foundation of his contribution to people of color, specifically the African Methodist Episcopal (AME) church and the United States in general.

Bishop Payne's educational roots are in the philanthropy and benevolence of free Black men in Charleston, SC. Through the organization, the Minors' Moralist Society (MMS), these professional men used their personal finances to educate orphan or indigent Black children. The organization consisted of 50 members, who each paid eight dollars per year to support this cause (Payne, 1968, p. 14). Bishop Payne was enrolled in one of the schools founded by the MMS at the age of eight. Receiving formal education until the age of 13, Bishop Payne then started two apprenticeships with a shoemaker and a carpenter. During his apprenticeship with the carpenter, Bishop Payne developed an ardent desire to read every book he could get his hands on, the first of which was the *Self-Interpreting Bible* by Rev.

John Brown (Payne, 1968, p. 15). Regarding his commitment to intellectual growth Bishop Payne recalled that: "I resolved to devote every moment of leisure to the study of books, and every cent to the purchase of them. I raised money by making tables, benches, clothes-horses, and corset-bones, which I sold on Saturday night in the public market." (Payne, 1968, p. 18)

Overall, Bishop Payne can be considered a self-educated man. His love for learning eventually inspired him, as a 19-year old free Black man, to abandon the carpentry trade and pursue the professional life of an educator. Bishop Payne served as an educator for approximately 10 years, until 1835, when he left South Carolina and journeyed to New York in search of a school for African Americans to lend his services. Instead, he was offered an opportunity to continue his formal studies at the Theological Seminary of the Presbyterian Church in Gettysburg, PA. While in seminary, Bishop Payne deepened his knowledge of Latin, Greek, Hebrew, Philosophy, Classics, and Systematic Theology (Payne, 1968, p. 59). However, after 2 years of training, he experienced an eye injury that prevented him from continuing his study and graduation. To supplement the remaining year of study, his professor and mentor Dr. S. S. Schmucker, provided Bishop Payne with a written recommendation to take to the AME church to be employed as a minister (Payne, 1968, p. 63). Bishop Payne then continued his formal education by learning a total of four languages: French, Latin, Hebrew, and Greek. Also, he authored numerous articles and sermons, and most notably he published the *History of the AME Church* (1891) and his autobiography, *Recollections of Seventy Years* (1881), ultimately earning honorary DD and LLD degrees for his life's work.

Professional Background

Bishop Payne's childhood and adulthood are proof of his dedication to education and earning an honest living. At the age of 13, he began work as an apprentice and at 14 he was under the care of a carpenter. Eventually at the age of 18 he developed and cultivated his passion for education. One of his first professional endeavors was to found a school for Black children and adults in his hometown of Charleston, SC. The names of the institutions Bishop Payne received his honorary degrees from are unknown. The name of the School Bishop Payne founded in Charleston, SC is unknown.

The school opened in 1829 with three children and three slaves at a fee of 50 cents per pupil. Bishop Payne was the only teacher in the school and taught as he learned. It gave him the opportunity to develop an educational model centered on experiential learning. Bishop Payne provides an example of his methods:

My researches in botany gave me a relish for zoology; but as I could never get hold of any work on this science I had to make books for myself. This I did by killing such insects, toads, snakes, young alligators, fishes, and young sharks as I could catch. I then cleaned and stuffed those that I could, and hung them upon the walls of my schoolroom. (Payne, 1968, p. 23)

The Charleston School's curriculum focused on reading, writing, arithmetic, grammar, botany, geography, and gymnastics. At the school's height, Bishop Payne enrolled approximately 50 students with varying educational levels. Unfortunately, the slave insurrection of 1831 by Nat Turner led to an increased discomfort of White Southern planters in South Carolina with the education of Black people. In addition, in December 1834, the South Carolina State Legislature passed Bill number 2639 prohibiting the education of slaves or persons of color (Payne, 1968, p. 27). Subsequently, Bishop Payne was forced to close his school in 1835. It was a great disappointment to Bishop Payne. Nevertheless, he used this setback as the motivation to advocate for the end of slavery.

Bill 2639 had a significant impact on Bishop Payne's life. It forced him to take a leave from his professional endeavors from 1835 until 1856 and to pursue his vocation as a minister in the AME church. Nevertheless, Bishop Payne maintained an ardent belief in the role of education to empower the Black community. He used education as a platform for ministerial reform in the AME church and ultimately for his greatest contribution, the founding of Wilberforce University.

Vocational Background

Bishop Payne from an early age maintained a desire to educate Black people. A statement by Bishop Payne that summarizes his joy of teaching is that: "My enthusiasm is the inspiration of my pupils" (Payne, 1968, p. 23). Bishop Payne undoubtedly believed that he was predestined by God to serve humanity in the capacity of an educator. He shares the recollection of his spiritual conversion below:

Several weeks after this event, between twelve and one o'clock one day, I was in my humble chamber, pouring out my prayers into the listening ears of the Saviour, when I felt as if the hands of a man were pressing my two shoulders and a voice speaking within my soul saying: "I have set thee apart to educate thyself in order that thou mayest be an educator to thy people." The impression was irresistible and divine; it gave a new direction to my thought and efforts. (Payne, 1968, p. 17)

This experience conveyed that God was directly involved in his affairs and motivated him with his efforts to found a school for the Black community of Charleston. When South Carolina prohibited the education of Black people, Bishop Payne travelled to New York City in search of opportunities to educate his people.

Upon his arrival, Dr. Martin suggested that he enroll in seminary as a scholarship recipient of the Society of Inquiry and Missions of the Lutheran Church. Bishop Payne's response to Dr. Martin is memorable:

> I told him that my highest aim was to be an educator; that the sanctities and responsibilities of the ministry were too great and awful for me. But he overcame my objections by showing the enlarged usefulness resulting from such a course, and stating that I would not be obliged to enter the ministry. (Payne, 1968, p. 45)

Bishop Payne was 15 years old when he reported his experience of the revelation of his vocation. In 1829 he set out to found the School in Charleston. In 1835, Bishop Payne journeyed to New York City. In the same year he accepted Dr. Martin's offer to study at the Lutheran Seminary with Dr. Schmucker. In 1838 Bishop Payne suffered a debilitating eye injury, which forced him to end his formal theological study. Dr. Schmucker gave him the following advice: "We should be glad to have you operate as a minister of the gospel in the Lutheran Church, but I think you can find a greater field of usefulness in the AME church; therefore, I advise you to join that body of professing Christians" (Payne, 1968, p. 61).

On the basis of this advice at hand, Bishop Payne volunteered his services to the AME church of Carlisle, PA. Shortly afterwards, in the midst of this service, he experienced another mystical encounter. Bishop Payne shared this experience: "After my misfortune came upon me I was lying upon my bed, lamenting and pondering over the future, when I felt a pressure from on high that constrained me to say with the Apostle Paul: 'Woe is me if I preach not the gospel'" (Payne, 1968, p. 62).

Accordingly, without delay, Bishop Payne engaged in suitable pursuits to enter the vocation of ministry. Departing Gettysburg in 1837, Bishop Payne arrived in Philadelphia, PA, with hopes of becoming an AME minister. However, he was advised not to join the Church because of growing disdain for educated clergy. After receiving this advice, Bishop Payne agreed to join the Franklin Synod of the Lutheran church and was licensed as a minister in June of 1837 and was ordained in 1839 (Payne, 1968, pp. 64–65). At the tender age of 26, Bishop Payne accepted the invitation of the Presbyterian church in East Troy, NY to serve as its pastor. Unfortunately, Bishop Payne fell ill again and due to his self-proclaimed overzealousness, he ruptured a throat gland and lost his voice for a year. This injury was followed by a severe cold which forced Bishop Payne to resign from his pastorate.

Once again, physical illness had impeded Bishop Payne's professional and vocational pursuits. In this instance, he returned to what he knew best; namely, being an educator. He relocated to Philadelphia, PA, in 1840 and opened a primary school for Black children. Bishop Payne shares his reflections:

> Soon after the holidays of 1839–40 I opened my school on Spruce Street, near Fourth. There were already two select schools in the city taught by white men, besides several primary schools. I began with three pupils (the same number with which I had opened in Charleston in 1830). At the end of the twelve months the two select schools emptied themselves into mine. Here I taught till the summer or 1843. (Payne, 1968, p. 72)

Bishop Payne's life was an orchestrated dance between life as an educator and that of a clergy, interrupted by an occasional waltz with illness. While founding his second school for Black children, Bishop Payne was in frequent contact with leaders of the AME church, specifically, Bishop Morris Brown, who served as his mentor. Under the influence of Bishop Brown, Bishop Payne joined the AME church in 1841, to become a local minister in 1842, and then be received as a full itinerate elder in 1843 (Payne, 1968, p. 74).

Following the function of his vocation, Bishop Payne left his post as an educator in June 1843 to assume the pastorate of Israel AME church in Washington, DC. Bishop Payne remained, for the next 13 years, as an itinerant minister of the AME church. He served as pastor of the Bethel AME church in Baltimore, MD (1845–1850). These years are significant in that Bishop Payne endured personal tragedy and battled with his first set of rejections in ministry. In 1847, Bishop Payne married his first wife Ms. Julia A. Ferris. Unfortunately, she died a year later during childbirth. Moreover, their prematurely born daughter lived for 9 months (Payne, 1968, p. 92). This personal tragedy came at a time when he was developing distinct pastoral idiosyncrasies.

Bishop Payne loved the process of planning, organizing, and preaching that came along with the pastorate; and, would even found his third school for Black children in Baltimore in 1846. However, he was often viewed as over pious and his desire for a culturally refined Black community led him to show displeasure for many aspects of slave culture that were incorporated into the church; namely, women in the pulpit and emotional liturgy. As an example, Bishop Payne spoke out against the "ring shout" and other songs that many Blacks embraced on the plantations. He called them "corn-field ditties" and thought it his responsibility to modify the worship experience in the AME church to resemble that of its White counterparts (Payne, 1968, p. 94).

In 1848, at the AME church General Conference, Bishop Payne was appointed the historiographer of the church. Having abandoned his charge to the Ebenezer Station AME church in Washington, DC, in 1850, he assumed full-time duties as church historian and travelled throughout the connection to gather all artifacts on the denomination. For 2 years, Bishop Payne travelled as far north as Canada, south to Florida, west to Louisiana, and east to Europe. His tasks were to collect every historical fact existing, which tells the story of the AME church, to collect minutes from meetings, letters of incorporation, financial and membership records, sermons and pamphlets produced by its leading members.

In fact, Bishop Payne's intellectual curiosity helped him produce the first history of the work of Black people in the United States. In the words of Bishop Payne: "During these two years of search for historical matter I supported myself by lecturing on economical subjects, such as, Industry and Thrift, The Springs of Wealth, and illustrated the lectures by maps." (Payne, 1968, p. 107)

In 1852, Bishop Payne's life was transformed by his election to the bishopric of the AME church at its general conference in Philadelphia, PA at Old Bethel AME Church. Bishop Payne claims that his nomination and election to the bishopric first occurred in 1848, when he was approached by Bishop Quinn to present his name. Bishop Payne declined this request and it seems that it was not offered to any other suitable candidate because no bishop was elected at this conference. However, in 1852, his name was offered without his knowledge and ministers in the church led by Bishops Quinn and Brown thought that he earned the right to be elevated to the office (Payne, 1888, pp. 109–110). He makes the following observation regarding this momentous event in his journal:

> On the 7th of May the election took place for two additional bishops. Votes were cast for Elders Richard Robinson, Augustus R. Green, Willis Nazrey, and D. A. Payne. The two latter were declared elected. I trembled from head to foot, and wept. I knew that I was unworthy of the office, because I had neither the physical strength, the learning; nor, the sanctity which makes one fit for such a high, holy, and responsible position. (Payne, 1888, p. 109)

Bishop Payne carried on his official duties until his death in 1884. He served as a bishop of the church for 42 years and made unprecedented life contributions to his beloved AME church that include: (a) creation of a minister's curriculum and requirements for pastoral training; (b) the creation of the organizational structure that includes Episcopal districts and annual conferences; (c) the expansion of the church into the west; (d) the creation of the publication arm of the church, including the *Christian Recorder* and the Sunday School Press; (e) the publication of the church hymnal; (f) the positioning of the church at the forefront of the antislavery movement; (g) the authorship of the church history; and (h) the founding of Wilberforce University and Payne Theological Seminary as part of the AME church.

Assumption of the Presidency of Wilberforce University

One of the hallmarks of English Methodism was the founding of educational institutions. English Methodism and American Methodism founded educational institutions and between the years of 1739 and 1850 both Methodism and the number of educational institutions grew in the United States. The AME church was well equipped to duplicate much of the administrative and missionary work of the church. However, it struggled to institute the fullness of John and Charles Wesley's Methodism because most of its founding ministers and the majority of its preachers were illiterate.

The education of the AME ministerial class and its congregations were major concerns of Bishop Payne. In 1833, under his urging, the Ohio Conference of the AME church made a historic request for an educational institution to be established by the Connection (the leaders and congregations of the AME). The resolution read:

> Resolved, 1st. As the sense of this house, that common schools, Sunday schools and temperance societies are of the highest importance to all people, but more especially to our people. Resolved, 2d. That it shall be the duty of every member of this Conference to do all in his power to promote and establish these useful institutions among our people. (Payne, 1969, p. 394)

This resolution led to the rise of a local movement in Ohio for increased literacy amongst the Black community and within the AME church as outlined in Chapter 3. Bishop Payne, who was then an itinerant minister in the Philadelphia Annual Conference and appointed the chair of the education committee in 1842 and 1843, presented a resolution to the AME church on the education of its clergy and laity. The resolution was adopted and read:

> Resolved, 2d. That we recommend to all our elders and deacons, licensed preachers and exhorters, the diligent and indefatigable study of the follow-

ing branches of useful knowledge, viz.: English grammar, geography, arithmetic, history, modern history, ecclesiastical history, natural and revealed
theology. (Payne, 1969, p. 395)

Under much opposition, these resolutions were fiercely debated in the
churches throughout the Connection, and more importantly with the pen
in the *African Methodist Episcopal Church Magazine*. Bishop Payne was at the
forefront of this movement as he composed his controversial *Epistles of Education* in which he articulated the need for an educated clergy. The editor
of the AME magazine commented: "Great fear is entertained by some that
if the measures proposed be adopted by the General Conference [of 1848],
discord and dissolution will necessarily take place in the Church between
the ignorant and the intelligent portions of it" (Payne, 1969, p. 396).

The excitement over Bishop Payne's epistles and subsequent educational movement reached its zenith in 1845 with the AME church's first
educational convention hosted by the Baltimore Conference. The convention granted the Connection an opportunity to hear arguments from both,
the proponents and opposition of the resolution. The convention resolved
to organize an educational association to educate young men for the ministry and to create the infrastructure and means to found an institution of
learning in the West and East. This resolution was a negotiated response
from the various opinions of the delegates. Given the lack of organization
and unity and the inability of one special interest group to fiscally support
entirely one of the resolutions adopted, the entire proposal failed.

Despite this failed effort, the Ohio Conference hosted a second education convention in September of 1845. Therein, they reported on the
success of a mission in Ohio in which they organized the Union Seminary.
Unfortunately, the seminary failed to attract the number of students and
qualified faculty needed to fulfill its mission and compete with the growing number of institutions founded with a similar purpose. In July 1856,
Bishop Payne relocated to Tawana Springs, Ohio with this second wife and
three step children as the presiding prelate of the area. During this time, he
became acquainted with several ministers of the Methodist Episcopal (ME)
church and their efforts to encourage the education of slaves and freedmen in Ohio. This school in Tawana Springs was dedicated and opened by
the ME church in October of 1856 and was named Wilberforce University
in honor of Mr. William Wilberforce an English statesman, philanthropist,
Christian, and abolitionist. The principal in charge of instruction was Mr.
M. P. Gaddis, a young Methodist preacher.

The curriculum included elementary school level English studies.
However, the White Trustees of the time believed Wilberforce to be a noble

experiment and incorporated it under the designation of university, despite its lack of academic credentials. Wilberforce University operated under the auspices of the ME church from 1856 until 1862. In addition to Mr. Gaddis, Mr. J. K. Parker and the Dr. R. S. Rust served as principal administrators (Payne, 1968, pp. 150–151). Unfortunately, as outlined in Chapter 3, the country was torn by Civil War in 1862.

Although the war officially ended in 1865 as a result of Lincoln's Emancipation Proclamation of April 1862, raising the finances required to support a school for slaves and freedmen was an increasingly difficult task. Financial challenges caused Wilberforce University of the ME church to close in June 1862. On March 10th, 1863, Bishop Payne received a notification about a trustee board meeting held in Cincinnati, OH to inform him of the executive committee's decision to sell the university. Having been forewarned, Bishop Payne immediately agreed to purchase the property on behalf of the AME church (Payne, 1968, p. 153). Accordingly, Bishop Payne was intimately involved with the institution since its inception. In his memoir, Bishop Payne (1881) reflects:

> In the first and original form his school was managed almost entirely by white persons. There were twenty-four trustees, of whom only four were men of color-viz.: Rev. Lewis Woodson, Mr. Alfred Anderson, Mr. Ishmael Keeth, and myself. Mr. Keeth attended but one meeting of the Board. . . . The only one of the trustees of color that aided in the actual management was myself, because, first, I was a member of the Executive Committee; second, I lived with my family on the college campus and had two step-children in the school; third, during the summer the white teachers and managers went away to recruit, and the establishment was left in my care during these months. (Payne, 1968, p. 226)

Bishop Payne and the trustees of the ME church agreed to sell Wilberforce University to the AME church for the sum of 10,000 dollars. Bishop Payne recollected on the purchase:

> The sum required was ten thousand dollars. When I made the bid for the property, I had not a ten-dollar bill at my command, but I had faith in God. Within forty-eight hours after that act a hundred dollars was given us by Mrs. James shorter, wife of Elder Shorter, and by June, 1863, we met the first payment of two thousand five hundred dollars. This sum was pledged and raised entirely by the Baltimore and Ohio Conferences. On the 11th of June Rev. James Shorter, Prof. John G, Mitchell, and myself consummated the arrangements for the purchase of Wilberforce University, and the title-deeds were handed to us as agents of the AME Church. It was then incorporated, a new charter taken out, and a new board of trustees elected. I was then elected to its Presidency. (Payne, 1968, p. 153)

What started in 1833 as an outgrowth of Bishop Payne's passion for education attainment and social justice for Black communities grew in 1856 to become a joint venture between the ME church and the AME church to start Wilberforce University. By 1863, this project had become the sole responsibility of the AME church and Bishop Payne was charged with its leadership. He served as president of the university until September 1, 1876, having given 20 years of dedicated service to ensuring that the institution fulfilled its mission of providing a quality education to the children of slaves and freedmen. Historically, Bishop Payne is recognized as the second administrator of Wilberforce University since its original founding in 1856 under the auspices of the ME church; the first president of the university under the auspices of the AME church; and the first Black president of a college or university in the United States. Bishop Payne is considered the first president of Wilberforce University of the AME church, as the leaders of the University under the control of the ME church appointed principals. The first principal was Rev. M. P. Gaddis, Jr. of the ME church. Bishop Payne was the first in the University's history to use the title, president (Gaustad, 1972, p. 3).

Educational Philosophy

Wilberforce University of the AME church maintained many of the aims developed while operating under the auspices of the ME church. The general mission of the university was Black community empowerment based on the premise that people of color must be the primary initiator, educator, and elevator of their own race in this and other lands (Payne, 1969, p. 428). The original charter of the institution stated:

> Hence, a leading object of the institution is to educate and thoroughly train many of them for professional teachers, or for any other position or pursuit in life to which God, in his providence or by his spirit may call them. (Payne, 1969, p. 428)

As president and Episcopal leader, Bishop Payne labored diligently to ensure that Wilberforce University adhered to the above standards. Curriculum was at the core of the university. Early in his career, as far back as his founding of the school in Charleston, Bishop Payne paid special attention to course offerings, as the means to train students to compete with their White counterparts, (b) grant them the ability to earn a sizable wage, (c) contribute to the overall positive perception of Black communities, and, (d) spread their knowledge throughout the United States and the world as ambassadors of a quality education.

As such, by 1865 Wilberforce's curriculum included English grammar and literature, Greek, Latin, lower mathematics, natural sciences, and French literature. By 1876 the university expanded into four departments: Theological Department (1866) offering a bachelor's of divinity degree (BD); Classical Department (1866) offering a bachelor's of arts degree (BA); Scientific Department (1867) offering a bachelor's of science degree (BS); and Normal Department (1872) offering a bachelor's of education degree (BE). Conferring these four degrees, Wilberforce University was considered a leader in Black education. Students flocked to the university with hopes of being transformed into civically minded, Christian oriented change agents, contributing to the personal and professional success of Black communities.

Vision, Goals, and Objectives

Bishop Payne's vision of a Wilberforce University was to position the AME church as a leader in the education of Black communities. He also viewed the singular mission of the institution to groom and prepare civically minded, Black, and Christian oriented change agents. This mission is reflected in the 1881 edition of the college catalogue: "The University aims to provide for students a liberal arts education, to give them the training necessary to make them fit for teaching others, or to fill with credit any position for which the various departments design them" (Wilberforce University College Catalogue of 1881).

Through its four divisions, Wilberforce University provided an academic foundation to many freedmen, and for those inclined an opportunity to enter the teaching profession or ministerial vocation. In the early years of Bishop Payne's tenure graduation was often a luxury for many of the students. Of the approximately 200 students who attended the university, only 29 are listed as graduates between the years of 1872 and 1876 (Payne, 1969, p. 430). Low graduation rates were due to a variety of factors the majority of which include the lack of financial resources to sustain a 2- or 3-year education and the urge to acquire basic skills and then return home to support families.

In the years of Reconstruction and the growing importance of education to the Black community, Bishop Payne focused on instilling strong moral character in his students. He believed that a quality education prepared students to effectively navigate the cultural nuances of American society. Much time was spent to ensure that each student adopted a robust Christian value system. The college catalogue outlined student requirements to include:

1. Proper observance of Sabbath—Attendance at Church Sabbath School; 2. Bathing and all preparations for Sabbath school must be attended to faithfully on Saturday evening; 3. Punctual attendance at prayers, recitations and other exercises; 4. Strict observance of the appointed study hours; 5. Every student will be held responsible for all improper conduct occurring in his room, and particularly accountable for any injury beyond ordinary use; 6. Every room must be accessible at all times to members of the Faculty; 7. Students must keep their rooms and dormitory halls in good order, and leave them clean at end of the term. All must assist in keeping the halls and school room clean and comfortable. (Wilberforce College catalogue of 1881)

Furthermore, students' moral development was reinforced by a rigid disciplinary system. Much of the code of conduct was to discourage inappropriate interactions with the opposite sex, alcoholism, vagrancy, absenteeism, damage to school property, and injury. Seemingly a very important issue, the catalogue also notes:

All unexcused delinquencies are registered, and when the number amounts to five, or any number higher than five, and less than ten, notice therefore is given to the student and his parent or guardian. When the number of unexcused delinquencies amounts to ten, the student ceases from being a member of the University. Any student, who marries while pursuing studies at the University, ceases to be a member of the same. (Wilberforce College catalogue of 1881)

Under the presidency of Bishop Payne, Wilberforce University reinforced the seriousness in pursuing a college education. Students had to prove a dedication to study, while sacrificing much of their desire for extracurricular activities. Any activity that could be categorized as play or leisure was often discouraged during the years of Bishop Payne's tenure. To fulfill its mission the university sought to discourage students from engaging in any activity that resembled plantation slave culture, such as, gambling, drinking, loitering, profanity, loud talking, and dancing. Students were encouraged to embrace their tenure at Wilberforce University as an opportunity that could not be wasted, requiring their full commitment and focus.

Accomplishments and Challenges

Bishop Payne worked vigorously to realize vision, mission, and goals of Wilberforce University. However, his relentless work and devotion were matched by some significant challenges. The four most significant challenges were: the burning of the original campus in 1865, encouraging the AME Connection to provide the necessary financial support, long-term faculty employment, and the continuous recruitment of students. Each of these obstacles shaped the institutional environment at Wilberforce University. These challenges ensued directly or indirectly from the fire of 1865. Bishop Payne (1891) writes:

> Everything indicated a prosperous future, when suddenly the buildings were set on fire by an incendiary. Within half an hour the building edifice was nothing but smoldering embers. The catastrophe fell upon us like a clap of thunder in a clear sky. It was a time of lamentation for our friends and rejoicing for our enemies. Said one of the latter: Now their buildings are burned, there is no hope for them. Another said: I wish lightning from heaven would burn down Wilberforce. This one supposed that his impious prayer was more than answered. But we believed and said: Out of the ashes of the beautiful frame building a nobler one shall arise. (Payne, 1969, pp. 429–430)

Bishop Payne with the collaboration of the entire university community managed to rebuild and record their most significant accomplishments: rebuilt the campus, organized a structure for management to guarantee efficiency and effectiveness, attracted a diverse donor base to support instruction, and produced a number of successful alumni. In his 1876 report, Bishop Payne detailed the university to own real estate in the amount of 53 acres of land, 10 of which were used for the campus. The ten acres included ten buildings, nine of which were cottages used for student and faculty housing. The main school house stood in the center of the campus and measured three stories tall. The university, after 1865, also boasted the addition of a library and small museum. During a most trying political and economic time, Bishop Payne led the university in raising over $50,000.00 from 1865–1876 (Payne, 1969, p. 435).

Not only was Bishop Payne a successful fundraiser, but he carved significant relationships based on his civic engagement that resulted in various types of contributions. Having enjoyed the audience of three U.S. presidents, including Abraham Lincoln, Bishop Payne also maintained a strong relationship with White Methodist organizations that still supported the work of Black education, despite their official separation from the university. In regards to President Lincoln, Bishop Payne was called to meet with him on the eve of the issuance of the Emancipation Proclamation to exchange views on the importance of freedom to Black people. He also maintained a close relationship with Maj. Gen. O. O. Howard of the Freedmen's Bureau, partnering with him to financially support the work of the university (Payne, 1881, pp. 144–150). Overall, the work of Bishop Payne continued at Wilberforce, Payne Theological Seminary, and within the AME church, through the education of ministers. They are living testaments to his conviction that education is essential to uplift of Black communities.

Education, employment, and land ownership helped the Robert family to enjoy an elite social status that continued throughout Reconstruction. With a rich and extensive cultural background, President Robert remained a prominent resident of Robertville until at least the 1850 U.S. census, in which he is listed as 40 years of age and employed as a Baptist minister. President Robert lived until 1884 and his posterity consisted of seven children, four boys and three girls. The family's legacy of civil service was carried on by his son Henry Martyn Robert. General Robert served the U.S. Army with distinction for 44 years. He retired in 1901 as the Brigadier General, Chief of Army Engineers. He is mostly remembered for revolutionizing parliamentary procedures through his publication—*Robert's Rule of Order* (1876).

Educational Background

President Robert continued his education at Furman Theological Seminary in 1832, where he studied for 2 years. Through these educational pursuits, President Robert was equipped to pursue his two passions; namely, education and theology.

Professional Background

President Robert developed a love for education at a young age. In 1850, he committed to this passion full time by accepting an offer to be a professor of mathematics and natural science at Burlington University in Des Moines, Iowa. President Robert left Burlington University in 1864 to assume the professor of languages chair at Iowa State University. He remained at Iowa University until 1869. President Robert then returned to Burlington University as its president. There are no historical artifacts available from this time in President Robert's career; however, a point that is consistently referenced is his deep-rooted disdain for the institution of slavery. Having grown up the son of a South Carolina planter, he was exposed to and witnessed firsthand the plight of Black people.

His conviction against slavery inspired him in 1871, upon the bequest of the American Baptist Home Mission Society, to be the first president (also cited as superintendent) of the Augusta Baptist Seminary, in Augusta, GA. In 1879 the Seminary was renamed the Atlanta Baptist Seminary, and in 1913 renamed Morehouse College.

Vocational Background

President Robert was licensed to preach in 1832 by the Baptist Church in Robertville and after completing 2 years of seminary training at Furman Theological Seminary was named pastor of the Baptist Church (Brawley, 1917, p. 22). President Robert carried on his passion for Christian ministry by pastoring churches around the country.

In 1839, he pastored the Baptist Church in Covington, KY. In 1841, he accepted the pastorate of the Baptist Church in Lebanon, KY. In 1848, he assumed leadership of the First Baptist Church in Savannah, GA and finally served in 1850, as pastor of the Baptist Church in Portsmouth, OH (Brawley, 1917, p. 22). For 18 years, President Robert remained actively involved in the itinerant ministry of the Baptist Church through his association with the American Baptist Home Mission Society. His continued work and commitment to the mission of this organization that guided the next 30 years of his professional and vocational life.

Assumption of the Presidency of Morehouse College

It was during his service to Burlington University that a movement to educate slaves and freedmen in the South began to take shape amongst the members of the American Baptist Home Mission Society (Society). Upon the request of the Society, following President Lincoln's issuance of the Emancipation Proclamation in April of 1862, Rev. H. C. Fish of New Jersey paid a visit to Washington, DC to report on the state of the newly freedmen. Rev. Fish's report claimed:

> The distinguishing traits of Immunity are nearly effaced. We had no idea of how near human beings may approximate to the brutes. Most of them have no more self-reliance or capacity for self-help, than children, and, have no idea of economy or accumulation. In some sense these contrabands are very religious people. They are excitable, impressible, and seemingly devout, in a very high degree and there is no doubt much real piety among them. But it often has with it a strange intermixing of ignorance and superstition and downright immorality.... Helpless, hopeless, friendless, these poor creatures appeal to us loudly for assistance. Not a man in the whole camp to care for their souls. Not a teacher to instruct them even in the lowest branches of learning. Difficult indeed is the problem. What are we to do for the freedmen, which are being thrown in increasing numbers upon our hands? One thing is certain they must not be neglected. And, upon whom else so clearly rest this obligation as upon the Baptists? (The American Baptist Home Mission Society (ABHMS), 1883, p. 398)

This report inspired in the Society's membership a sense of moral responsibility to come to the aid of the freedmen. In September 1863, the Society's board voted to approve a new initiative to support the empowerment of the freedmen in the South:

> The definite purpose and policy is to send assistants to our missionaries in the South to engage in such instruction of the colored people as will enable them to read the Bible and to become self-supporting and self-directing churches. The Board will gladly receive all moneys contributed and designated for this purpose and appropriate the same agreeably to the wishes of the donors the moneys thus designated to be termed the Freedmen's Fund. (ABHMS, 1883, p. 399)

This resolution led the Society to engage in extensive efforts to educate freedmen. These mission fields were located in Virginia, North Carolina, South Carolina, Louisiana, Tennessee, and Georgia. The Society sent zealous missionaries who were to aid existing churches and Baptist organizations with the creation of schools and other means to assist freedmen.

Unfortunately, this aid was not received with the highest esteem by White southern planters in the South. As the country was increasingly torn by Civil War, regional sentiments and class loyalties divided the Baptist church and had a negative impact on the work of the Society.

Ultimately, the Northern Society was forced to publicly express its support of the Union, and denounce its Southern brethren. In a resolution made by the Society to President Lincoln and the Secretary of State in 1863 they proclaimed:

> Resolved, 3rd. That we rejoice in the interest manifested by the national authorities in the establishment of schools and the reconstruction of Christian institutions throughout the recovered portions of the Southern land as an evidence of their practical recognition of the Gospel as the only sure basis and the best safeguard of public peace and prosperity and that we hereby offer them our most cordial thanks for the facilities afforded to our own as well as to kindred organizations in the prosecution of this momentous work. Resolved, 4th. That however prolonged may be the conflict and whatever it cost our trust in the final triumph of liberty and righteousness remains unshaken and that equally in defeat as in victory we hold fast to the conviction that a merciful though chastening God will in His own time bring forth from the carnage and woe of this civil war a brighter grander future for our country and the world. (ABHMS, 1883, p. 401)

This final attempt to bring unity to the Society and the Baptist churches in the North and South in support of their mission work among the newly freedmen was a short-term success. The Society by its annual meeting in 1865 counted 63 workers employed in the South and $4,978.69 in total funds deposited into the Freedmen's Fund (ABHMS, 1883, p. 402). Despite this noticeable accomplishment, the Society still struggled with differing opinions about the best ways to meet the challenges of freedmen in the South by its Northern Baptists and continued resistance to the empowerment of the freedmen by Southern Baptists. To address these concerns, at its 1865 annual meeting, the members of the Society voted and approved the following resolution:

> Resolved, That the Society will expect of its Executive Board that undeterred by any impracticable strict construction they should feel themselves bound to carry into effect in all wise and feasible ways the evangelization of the freedmen and to aid them in the erection or procurement of Church and school edifices when requisite. Resolved, That the Society will expect of all churches and associations connected with it a vigorous and hearty cooperation not only in raising the funds needed in the present exigency but also in commending to the Board for employment such fitting instruments—preachers, colporteurs and teachers—male and female as they know to be well qualified and faithful. (ABHMS, 1883, p. 404)

Each of the previous resolutions laid the necessary groundwork for the validation of what was then called the National Theological Institute (NTI) to be associated with, guided, and to be a recipient of substantial financial support by the Society. NTI was founded in 1863 in Washington, DC by a small group of Society members and was one of the mission fields held in contempt by White Southern Baptist members for maintaining an over aggressive mission and purpose. NTI, led by Rev. Edmund Turney, served as the parent organization of a network of theological seminaries throughout the South. There were campuses in Richmond, VA and in Augusta, GA. The campus in Augusta was called the Augusta Institute (Brawley, 1917, p. 14). It was short lived given that the work of NTI was formerly merged with that of the Society in 1869 and the management and administration of the Augusta Institute fell under the direction of the Society.

The Augusta Institute was officially founded in 1867 as part of the NTI charter. Under the commission and authority of Dr. Turney, Mr. Richard C. Coulter, a freeman of extreme resourcefulness, returned to Augusta to begin the work of building a seminary. Mr. Coulter, though equipped with the zeal for such a task, did not feel himself to possess the other skills and talents necessary. He then requested the assistance of the Rev. William J. White, a local undertaker, to lead the effort. By September of 1866, Rev.

White secured a partnership with the Springfield Baptist Church and had enrolled 37 students (Brawley, 1917, pp. 13–14).

The first challenge to overcome was the selection of an able teacher. Dr. Turney authorized Rev. White to teach; however, the latter felt it outside the scope of his expertise. During their search for an adequate teacher, Rev. White was appointed an agent of the Freedmen's Bureau and assigned to traveling over Georgia.

After assuming his post, he consulted with a colleague in the American Missionary Association (AMA), and as a result in February 1867, three female Baptist teachers began instruction at the institute (Brawley, 1917, p. 16). Over the next 3 years, the institute faced threats from the KKK, increased student attrition, frequent turnover in leadership, and lack of adequate resources (Rovarius, 2005, p. 56). In an effort to chart a new course for the institute, Rev. White and his colleagues sought the aid of a recognized and skilled educator and administration to take leadership of the seminary as its first president. In 1871, the Society was successful in securing the services of the Rev. Dr. Joseph T. Robert; and, in the Fall of that year he assumed the presidency. He served as president until his death in 1884.

Educational Philosophy

President Robert worked diligently to fulfill the mission of the Society and the Augusta Institute. In compliance with the mission of the Society, his goals were: (a) general missionary work in winning men to Christ and gathering them into churches secular education, (b) to enable the people to read the Bible, and, (c) the education of ministers through ministers' classes at central points (ABHMS, 1883, p. 405). These goals were codified in the following resolution:

> In carrying on and extending that portion of their work which has already given instruction to more than three hundred colored brethren engaged in the ministry; or, having it in view, as equally demanded by the exigencies of the Society, whose great object is to promote the preaching of the Gospel in every part of the land; and, also bidding God speed to any similar or affiliated institution having in view the same or kindred objects. (ABHMS, 1883, p. 407)

The Augusta Institute aimed to educate preachers and teachers. Moreover, as of 1871 women were no longer allowed to enter into the class, and the Augusta Institute began its commitment to the education of men. No specific reason is given for this decision by President Robert. However, the

ABHMS and the Southern Baptist organization were known for not supporting the religious training of women for the ministry. The ABHMS history states:

> We need missionary cooks, dressmakers and housekeepers. We need a tenfold augmentation of the blessed activity of our Woman's Home Mission Society. We cannot overestimate the importance of the work which the Florence Nightingales under its care are doing for the colored women of the South in their missions of mercy amid the dirt and degradation of the Negro quarters. (ABHMS, 1883, p. 271)

This principle is used to justify the decision. In addition, President Robert eliminated the instruction of men younger than 16 years. Thus, the institute developed a reputation for its focus on the education of adult males to become teachers and preachers.

The curricular instruction of the institute prior to 1871 was similar to that of a typical school of the time period. College level work occurred at a minimum, given that many of the students possessed limited educational skills and abilities. To overcome this challenge, President Robert formulated a curriculum that prepared students for college level work, while ensuring that the more advanced students received a liberal arts education comparable to institutions across the country. Herein, the range of studies at this time were very broad, comprising elementary level competencies such as reading and writing; and, the more advanced students received instruction in algebra, geometry, physiology, botany, natural philosophy, rhetoric, Latin, and New Testament Greek. Exercises in declamation and composition were required once a week (Brawley, 1917, p. 28).

From 1871 to 1883 the institute sought to prepare Black men for the ministry; however, none of the students officially graduated from the course of study. It seems that major educational focus of the students enrolled was to receive adequate education to prepare them for international mission work under the auspices of the Society or the AMA. With this ministry focus, President Robert emphasized an intense concentration on Christian education. He prided himself on providing students with the educational foundation and oratory skills needed to deliver soul-stirring and content-rich sermons throughout the city, nation, and the world. As part of their co-curricular experience, students took an active part in the work of the Sunday schools of the city and surrounding country. The preachers were much sought after to speak in the city churches. They were often tempted to preach more than President Robert advised (Brawley, 1917, p. 29).

Despite his best efforts to encourage students to spend more time in the classroom, they continued to develop a reputation for their grasp of the Bible and their ability to articulate its meanings. During the early part of his tenure President Robert was opposed to this reputation. He sought to establish an academically rigorous educational setting; however, prospective students were attracted to the institute because of the oratory skills of the attendees. Thus, he learned to accept the reputation and he continued to work to raise academic standards. To President Robert's credit, the institute earned a reputation for producing high caliber Black ministers and ultimately national recognition for the quality of its education.

The institute struggled to make sure that each minister enrolled received the education necessary to perform his duties. This unevenness in students' skills levels resulted in constant problems throughout President Robert's tenure. On one hand, the successful recruitment of teachers increased the reputation of the institute, which attracted students who either lacked an understanding of the fundamentals or were interested in using their newly acquired intellectual prowess to chase after money, women, and the dreams of high culture in Southern society afforded to ministers of the day (Brawley, 1917, pp. 41–42). On the other hand, President Robert and the faculty's continued commitment to academic excellence, while assisting the men to form accurate and productive world views and while completing their undergraduate studies, led to the first degrees being conferred in May 1884.

Vision, Goals, and Objectives

President Robert's vision was to develop Augusta Institute into a well-respected 4-year liberal arts college in the United States that equips Black men with the skills, tools, and competencies to be successful ministers and teachers, and exemplars of the transformational powers of a quality higher education. President Robert committed himself to this vision throughout his professional and vocational career. His tenure at the Augusta Institute allowed him to fulfill this ideal. To understand the full impact of his presidency on the seminary, one must consider its state prior to his arrival. The whole enterprise was looked upon with extreme disfavor by most of the White people in the community. The buildings were dilapidated and in need of repairs. Furthermore, these buildings contained no furniture or equipment, beside nails in the walls and a few books on a bench. There was considerable debt and no funding sources in place to assist (Brawley, 1917, p. 23).

Despite the state of the institution in 1871, President Robert embarked on an ambitious plan to create what is viewed today as the most prominent institution for the training of Black men in the world. On the basis of his ideal, he realized the following goals: (a) use the institute's association with the Society to raise funds for capital projects and the support of the most intellectually advanced students; (b) partner with the Black Baptist churches in the community to increase enrollment and support of institutional needs; (c) create an organizational structure that sustains growth; and (d) emphasize the importance of developing practical experience, creating local mission fields through civic engagement opportunities, internships, and work opportunities for students.

Accomplishments and Challenges

As listed in the previous section, early in his career, President Robert developed a deep appreciation for Black higher education and was religiously committed to the preparation of Black ministers and teachers. To build Augusta Institute into a competitive educational institution, he had to improve fundraising strategies, the physical plant, student quality, and administrative structure and practices to show special skills for development. In so doing, he faced quite a few challenges, while achieving many more accomplishments.

In the context of the time, raising funds amongst White Southern Baptist churches was virtually impossible. Even with the support of the Society and after writing over 100 letters to the brethren in Georgia and New Hampshire, President Robert understood the success of the institute had to be placed squarely on the shoulders of the community it would most benefit—the Southern Black Baptist churches. Thus, he made a systematic and straightforward appeal to their sense of community pride and the need to invest in their future. With consistent annual fundraising stratagems President Robert was able to raise funds, amongst Whites and Blacks that provided for the repairs to the buildings, purchase of schoolroom and bedroom furniture, hiring of administrative staff and faculty, and payment of operational costs (Brawley, 1917, p. 24). These contributions and President Robert's political shrewdness eventually led to a book donation which contained 503 volumes, two $50 pledges, two $100 gifts, and the establishment of scholarships by the New York State Colonization Society and other private donors (Brawley, 1917, pp. 26–27).

President Robert's fundraising success overflowed into improved facilities, increased enrollment, and earned the institution the respect of the White and Black community for its progress. However, President Robert was dissatisfied. He thought it necessary to revamp the institute completely. He initiated this feat in planning the acquisition of a new campus and orchestrated an administrative reorganization. The major issue facing the institute in 1880 was the inability to grow. By 1878 there were 245 men enrolled as pupils, 150 of these men were ministerial students. The cost of tuition per student was $12 annually. Certainly, the money generated could not sustain the institution. The only option was to increase student enrollment.

President Robert turned to his friends at the Society and after much negotiations in 1879 the Society approved $12,500 to transfer the Augusta school to Atlanta and to purchase a site along with the erection of a building (ABHMS, 1883, p. 410). Some unexpected challenges grew around the expansion of the institute and the erection of the new site. There was an additional $4,000 debt, increased operational cost, increased noise, uncomfortable accommodations, and lack of dormitory space (Brawley, 1917, pp. 35–36). Thus, in 1882, President Robert secured an additional $17,500 from the Society for the purchase of additional buildings for the Atlanta school to accommodate student housing and other needs (ABHMS, 1883, p. 414). Upon the relocation of the institute from Augusta to Atlanta in 1879, President Robert realized that the institute needed to enhance its managerial and fiscal effectiveness. The only way to achieve this goal was to implement a new organizational structure. He thus petitioned the Society to allow renaming the institute as the Atlanta Baptist Seminary. The Society's position is reflected in the following statement:

> Early in 1881 the Board reorganized the Southern work, so that effort shall be conducted chiefly in cooperation with of colored Baptists or white Baptists, while the Superintendents of the schools shall devote attention each year to the holding of institutes...As the colored people of the South become more intelligent better organized and more able to cultivate their own field, services of a superintendent of missions are not as necessary as they were twenty or even ten years earlier. (ABHMS, 1883, p. 414)

By moving the Institute Society to a more decentralized administrative policy in 1881, President Robert in 1879 carried out the foresight needed to lead this institution. In April 1879, the reincorporation was completed, along with a revision of the by-laws of the board of trustees in July 1879. Each of the previous actions assisted the seminary with increasing its student population and the size of physical plant. They also enhance its managerial and fiscal effectiveness. More importantly, the reorganization positioned the newly formed Black organization, the Negro Baptist Education Society, to play an integral role in the educational development of the Black community through the seminary. The statements published by the trustees best summarize the legacy of President Robert:

When the subject of assuming the delicate and responsible position of the presidency of what is now known as the Atlanta Baptist Seminary was presented to him, it was considered in the light of duty, and in accepting it he brought into his work, with the experience and culture of a lifetime, all the enthusiasm of an ardent nature sanctified by divine grace. To this wisdom, tact, and energy displayed by him in the management of the Seminary is due, under the favor of God, the prosperous condition in which he left it and the present hopeful outlook for its future usefulness. (Brawley, 1917, p. 38)

The contributions of President Robert to Black higher education in the United States are undeniable. It is common knowledge that every major endeavor has its challenges. And, certainly, the seminary faced many challenges. However, President Robert met each challenge with resolve and a faith in his commitment to developing Black men's intellectual talents.

Conclusion

These two founding presidents, the Rt. Rev. Dr. Daniel A. Payne and the Rev. Dr. Joseph T. Robert, are both men of character, wisdom, intellect, and above all committed to Black higher education. A single thread weaves together the accomplishments of these two men—the legacies of their life-works at Wilberforce University and Morehouse College. Moreover, these men were not just educational leaders; they were both religious leaders, each sharing pastoral vocational backgrounds and a corresponding commitment to Christian education.

They were born 4 years apart. President Robert was born in 1807 and Bishop Payne in 1811. Both presidents were born in the state of South Carolina, traveled to the West and forged great relationships in the North. They used their gifts to realize the educational goals of religious organizations. Moreover, they came of age as men, spiritual leaders, and educational leaders during one of the most difficult periods of U.S. history, the Civil War. They grew in the shadow of slavery. Each president lived a life of service dedicated to the emancipation of the mind, body, and soul of Black men and women. Bishop Payne dedicated 11 years and President Robert dedicated 13 years. Finally, both these great men left for the hosts of students, colleagues, family, friends, and admirers the treasures of wisdom and knowledge to effectively lead a historically Black educational institution.

Note

1. The Huguenots were French Protestants most of whom eventually came to follow the teachings of John Calvin, and who, due to religious persecution, were forced to flee France to other countries in the 16th and 17th centuries.

5

Institutional Comparisons, 1865–1884

This chapter uses an institutional assessment model that includes a demographical and mission-based comparison of the respective college to assess each president's impact and influence on their respective institutions. It uses James Alan Laub's institutional assessment model.

Educational Leadership Laub's (2000) Servant Leadership Traits

Dr. Laub's model consists of six categories which will be used to evaluate the servant leadership values of Bishop Payne and President Robert and their corresponding organizational precepts which shaped Wilberforce University and Atlanta Baptist Seminary (Morehouse). The six leadership values that should guide a servant leader are:

1. Value people (the leader's ability to believe in people, serve others' needs prior to their own, and participate in receptive, nonjudgmental listening).

Not For Ourselves Alone, pages 91–114
Copyright © 2019 by Information Age Publishing
All rights of reproduction in any form reserved.

2. Develop people's abilities (the leader's ability to provide opportunities for learning and growth, model appropriate behavior, and use encouragement to build others). Build relationships (the leader's ability to cultivate strong personal relationships, work collaboratively, and value differences).
3. Display authenticity (the leader's ability to be open and accountable, willingness to learn from others, and maintain integrity and trust).
4. Provide leadership (the leader's ability to envision the future, take initiative, and clarify goals).
5. Share leadership (the leader's ability to facilitate a shared vision, share power by releasing control, and share status by promoting others).

Assessing Servant Leadership Values

Dr. Laub's (2000) servant leadership model provides an assessment framework to measure the historical impact of Bishop Payne and President Robert's servant leadership characteristics and that of their respective institutions. Greenleaf (1998) developed servant leadership in reflections on the state of affairs at colleges and universities in the United States during the 1960s (pp. 20–21). It is thus appropriate to determine whether or not these leadership traits are operative in the leadership styles of college and university presidents.

In the case of Bishop Payne and President Robert, this study extends the servant leadership paradigm to assess a parallel historical period. Approximately one century earlier, the works of these founding presidents were among historical Black and Christian-centered colleges. Since there are no living subjects to qualitatively assess the leadership of these presidents, this study relies on the various historical artifacts collected: college histories, catalogues, speeches, memoirs, and other primary source materials. The goal is to identify and evaluate the narratives of accomplishments and challenges faced by the presidents by analyzing and assessing these data in search of evidence pointing to the use of any servant leadership traits identified by Dr. Laub (2000).

This investigation is carried out through five categories to draw the role of servant leadership traits in the leadership styles of Bishop Payne and President Robert. These categories are: (a) commitment to higher education, (b) value of Christian education, (c) support and development of students, (d) character development and staff support, and (e) cultivating meaningful relationships. Once it has been determined whether or not Bishop Payne and President Robert possessed these servant leadership traits, a sixth category will be developed to assess the impact of Laub's categories on the leadership of Bishop Payne and President Robert. Specifically, this category is called vision-setting and implementation.

Commitment to Higher Education

A key characteristic that should guide every quality college administrator is a commitment to higher education. From those who work in student affairs to those who manage academic concerns, the common trait held by each must be a commitment to education in general, and higher education specifically. The term commitment to education is best understood as a belief in the value of cultural transmission. Jerome Bruner (1996) explained that culture shapes minds, that it provides us with the tool kit by which we construct not only our worlds, but our very conceptions of ourselves and our abilities (Bruner, 1996). Certainly, Bishop Payne and President Robert each developed into educational leaders as a result of unique cultural experiences and these experiences led to a superior commitment to education.

Bishop Payne from his earliest days, as shown in Chapter 4, witnessed the power of education via its use by White slave owners to maintain their social, political, and economic superiority. In his autobiography, Bishop Payne recounts being petitioned by a wealthy slaveholder, who was looking for a young Black man to manage his personal affairs in the West Indies, commenting:

> I was commended to him, and called upon him at the Planters' Hotel. Among the inducements he offered he said: "If you will go with me, the knowledge that you will acquire of men and things will be of far more value to you than the wages I will pay you. Do you know what makes the difference between the master and the slave? Nothing but superior knowledge." (Payne, 1888, p. 19)

These comments from the wealthy slave owner ignited in Bishop Payne a passion for education. These also defined for him the importance of education and elevated its prestige over riches and fame. Bishop Payne committed himself to obtaining an education with the conviction that it would afford him the ability to escape the slave status of his foreparents and positively change the social oppression of his immediate environment.

Bishop Payne educated himself and was dedicated to the education of others. From his early adulthood, Bishop Payne sought the media to provide educational opportunities: founding three elementary schools in

Charleston, SC; Philadelphia, PA; and Baltimore, MD. A relentless pursuit for intellectual stimulation is the best definition of Bishop Payne's thirst for knowledge. Describing this thirst, he writes:

> At the same time with geography I studied and mastered English grammar. I began with Murray's *Primary Grammar,* and committed the entire book to memory, but did not understand it; so, I reviewed it. Then light sprung up; still I felt like one in a dungeon who beheld a glimmer of light at a distance, and with steady but cautious footsteps moved toward it, inspired by the hope that I would soon find its source and come out into the full blaze of animated day. (Payne, 1888, p. 21)

It is noteworthy that Bishop Payne's commitment to education was supported by his conviction that he was set apart by God to be an educator. To be committed to education was also a commitment to his divine purpose (Payne, 1888, p. 17). Bishop Payne would carry out this purpose through his Episcopal service as the President of Wilberforce University and a leader in the AME church and demanding others to empower themselves through the attainment of a quality education.

These events signify that Bishop Payne was authentic about his purpose and was willing to take the necessary steps to realize his goal of helping to build the Black community through the development of their intellect. As president, he emphasized education as a social responsibility of parents towards children and an inheritance prepared for children by their parents. Bishop Payne wrote regarding the importance of education to the development of the race:

> But of the children take special care. Heaven has entrusted them to you for a special purpose. What is that purpose? Not merely to eat and to drink, still less to gormandize. Not merely to dress finely in broadcloths, silks, satins, jewelry, nor to dance to the sound of tambourine and fiddle; but to learn them how to live and how to die to train them for great usefulness on earth—to prepare them for great glory in heaven. Keep your children in the schools, even if you have to eat less, drink less and wear coarser raiment; though you eat but two meals a day, purchase but one change of garment during the year, and relinquish all the luxuries of which we are so fond, but which are as injurious to health and long life as they are pleasing to the taste. Let the education of your children penetrate the heart. (Sernett, 1985, p. 220)

As a Bishop, he challenged pastors, parishioners, and colleagues to acquire as much education as they could and support the founding of educational institutions in their local communities. Bishop Payne believed that an educated priestly class in the Black community would result in the elevation of the Black race, as a whole. Ministers should teach not only from their experience, but from the knowledge acquired through higher educational institutions, ultimately rivaling their White counterparts in the mastery of history, grammar, math, and science. Bishop Payne equated education to cultural refinement, quality of life, and Christian service.

President Robert was also committed to education. His educational pursuit of a doctor in medicine degree is proof that he held education in high esteem. Moreover, President Robert did not have to use education as a vehicle of personal transformation, having been born to a family of means and social status. A member of a privileged community, he first sought a career as a medical doctor; nevertheless, he chose to pursue a career in education and the vocation of ministry. Even though no information is available that directly explains his change in career choice, President Robert remarked that, even from a young age, he opposed slavery.

Despite the lack of historical artifacts about this period of President Robert's life, much of the cultural influences of that day can be ascertained by examining his life journey. Following his life travels, he resided in the states of Washington, Rhode Island, Georgia, Kentucky, Iowa, and Ohio. Of the states cited, only Kentucky was chosen for a reason other than education, only to assume a pastorate. Additionally, President Robert only lived in three southern states in which he was exposed to the ills of slavery as a young man and pastor. No record exists of the experiences that shaped his young adult life, other than what we know about 19th century U.S. history referenced in Chapter 3. Thus, this time period provides the cultural context that shaped his perspective and influenced his life choices.

Completing an undergraduate degree at Brown University, graduate work at Yale University, doctoral work at South Carolina Medical College, and theological study at Furman Theological Seminary, President Robert was shaped and molded by Northern liberal republican Baptist ideals. Of particular interest was the time President Robert spent at Furman Theological Seminary from 1832 to 1834. During these years this seminary was a struggling institution, which enrolled approximately 12 students in 1830. With Robert's enrollment in 1832 the number of total students enrolled is unknown. However, it is accepted that the institution was located in the house of the principal, Rev. Jesse Hartwell. Principal Hartwell taught and trained the students. He was employed by the Baptist convention to make the theological department most prominent. Furman Theological Seminary experienced numerous challenges; its finances were the most pressing and in 1834 closed its doors for a time (Furman University: History, 1830–1839, paras. 1–5).

Education, for President Robert, was a vehicle by which he developed his academic, ideological, and religious training in preparation for service. However, it was also influential in shaping his perspective of educational leadership and the role of higher education in creating a generation of Baptist ministers. Witnessing firsthand the development of Brown University, the intellectual vigor of Yale University, the prejudices of South Carolina Medical College, and the struggles of Furman Theological Seminary, he was also exposed to the important mission of higher education throughout the United States. He understood the commitment needed to lead an educational institution as a social justice institution. These events point to President Robert's mission to build and support Black male preachers, inspiring in them the desire to refine their intellects to eventually assume leadership positions in the Black community.

Bishop Payne and President Robert both believed in the transformative power of education. They both acquired advanced degrees. Bishop Payne was primarily self-taught, while President Robert attended some of the most prestigious institutions in the United States. Bishop Payne discovered his passion to be an educator from an early age, and immediately began living out his dream. President Robert desired to be a doctor, and then through pastoral service evolved into an educator. Education, for Bishop Payne, was a divine calling, a means by which he could work to uplift his race. Commitment to education, for President Robert, was the natural implication of his desire to escape slave culture in the South. For both, education was a means by which they could improve their social context. Through their relentless pursuit to erect exemplary institutions of higher learning for the Black communities, they show evidence of the servant leadership traits by valuing people, developing people, building people, and sharing leadership.

The Value of Christian Education

Nineteenth century U.S. history is rich with numerous occurrences that defined the many aspects of American culture. From the Civil War to Reconstruction, agrarian political economies to capitalistic market economies and industrialization, the ratification of the U.S. Constitution to the assassination of President Lincoln, the fugitive slave laws to emancipation and the Black codes; during these periods, the United States experienced more changes than ever before. One outcome of these social, economic, and political changes was the rise in secularism. This cultural shift granted Americans increased freedom and technology. In response to this increased secularization between 1800 and 1830, the United States experienced its Second Great Awakening.

Coming out of this second revival movement was the birth of the Bible College movement, which in turn sparked the beginning of Christian Education, which is still prevalent (Anthony & Benson, 2003, p. 316). These revival experiences created a thirst for biblical knowledge to confront the cultural changes of the time. Leaders of all Protestant denominations in the United States were called upon to create schools, colleges, and seminaries to train a new generation of moral and ethical Christian leaders. William G. McLoughlin (1978) reflects:

> These early religious awakenings had a major impact on the development of Christian education in Protestant churches. The awakening themselves were educational experiences for adults and to a lesser degree for children. In their tent meetings religious awakenings took to task not only the quality of religious observance but the existing educational methods of producing so-called committed Christians. (p. 161)

Bishop Payne was ordained in the AME church in 1843, and President Robert was ordained in the Baptist Church in 1832. Given the spirit of their time, they were certainly influenced by the revival movement to have a firm belief in the necessity of Christian education. As presidents, they developed and maintained a commitment to not just higher education, but Christian higher education and the preparation of ministers as well. In their efforts to promote Christian education, the AME church asked each of its conferences to establish education committees to advance the cause through the creation of Sunday schools, secondary schools, and colleges. A report from the Ohio Conference, in which Wilberforce University was a member, noted:

> On a religious education we cannot place too high an estimate, as it is of the most vital importance to all. And here we would remark, that we mean by religious education the religion of the Lord Jesus Christ, the regeneration of the spirit, the sanctification of life, and the purifying of the affections. This qualifies for every duty in life. Religious education should always keep pace with the intellectual, in order to produce a well-balanced mind. (Payne, 1891, p. 403)

Clearly, the AME church understood the importance of Christian education in the development of exemplary men and women. These views were entirely in unison with the mission of Wilberforce University. The college catalogue of 1881 identifies a moral code of conduct for all students, and outlines requirements for religious observance and Christian service. These expectations were inherent to the very fabric of the institution. The admission criteria integrated the standards for moral and religious education.

The catalogue of Wilberforce University reinforced that: "Divinity students must come to us fully endorsed by the church authorities as possessing gifts, graces and fruits; otherwise they will not be permitted to enter the Theological Department, and will be put on trial according to the 10th cannon of the AME Church." (Wilberforce University, 1881, College Catalogue, p. 32)

Moreover, Wilberforce University's curriculum included daily religious exercises as a component of its students' religious education through mandatory daily religious exercises. Under the heading "Religious Instruction" the catalogue states:

> At 7:45 a.m. and at 4 p.m. all the pupils gather in the chapel for religious devotion which consists in reading a portion of the Scriptures, singing a hymn, and a prayer; at which all are required to be present. These exercises have a most happy influence on the pupils, and have done much in making the labors of governing comparatively light. (Wilberforce University, 1881, College Catalogue, p. x)

It is remarkable that Wilberforce University expected from its students, while on campus, to lead a rigorous contemplative lifestyle as a form of religious instruction. Additional requirements are listed in the catalogue under the heading: "Prohibitions and Requirements" that detailed various behaviors considered acceptable. Religious (Christian) education was an important aspect of campus culture, and viewed by Bishop Payne as a critical support to the overall administration of the university. He believed that if students were trained to honor God, they would naturally honor themselves, and their social neighbors. Certainly, these efforts to train students to adopt the highest moral and ethical standards displays authenticity and shared leadership. The servant leadership traits that develop and build people are also present, even though students may not have been willing, as evidenced through the penalties for bad conduct. Nevertheless, through the infrastructure and curriculum of Wilberforce University, Bishop Payne fostered a culture for students to develop into servant leaders.

Atlanta Baptist Seminary was founded with a similar commitment to Christian education. As shown in Chapter 4, upon President Robert's assumption of the leadership of Augusta Institute (renamed Atlanta Baptist Seminary in 1879) the College was led by local and/or traveling ministers, the instruction staff consisted of female missionaries, while it was housed in the Springfield Baptist Church. It was then relocated to a recently purchased poorly suited school house; during this period, its curriculum was uneven because it was based on the vastly different skills of the enrolled students. President Robert worked to organize the institution using the

American Baptist Home Mission Society's (ABHMS) educational mission as its focus.

A unique aspect of the seminary was President Robert's focus on Christian service. Under President Robert's tenure, the seminary created a niche to train Black male ministers for pastorates and mission work. Thus, Christian education was the key objective of an Atlanta Baptist Seminary education. With this ministry focus, President Robert ensured that faculty concentrated on preparing these men to be high caliber Christian leaders with remarkable intellect and moral standards. He prided himself in providing students with the educational foundation and oratory skills to deliver soul-stirring and content-rich sermons throughout the city, nation, and the world. As part of their co-curricular experience, students took an active part in the work of the Sunday schools of the city and surrounding country. The preachers were much sought after to speak in the city churches; and, they were often tempted to do more of this work than President Robert advised (Brawley, 1917, p. 29, p. 120).

By concentrating on service learning, President Robert displayed concern for the development of students into academicians and servant leaders. Requiring their participation in community activities, he developed a culture of authenticity, shared leadership, and instilled in students a sense of self-pride and motivated them to continue in their educational pursuits. The success of the seminary under President Robert's leadership is a testament to this ability to engage students intellectually and personally. His personal touch helped students develop pastoral sensibilities and a commitment to Christian education and mission. President Robert instilled this appreciation for the art of teaching the Bible and preaching through Monday evening meetings with students to report on their missionary activities. He held Wednesday evening Literary Society meetings to discuss the latest books and debated their impact on their work. Brawley (1917) writes:

> Supplementing their course of study, from very early years the student labored for self-cultivation. In 1880–1 there were two well organized societies, the Missionary Society that met once a week for the general promotion of home missions, and the Ciceronian Lyceum that met every other week for practice in extemporaneous speaking and parliamentary usage. The students also held a prayer meeting every Wednesday night. (Brawley, 1917, p. 120)

The seminary's commitment to Christian education is further illustrated in President Robert's ability to communicate a shared vision to trained ministers. This fact is shown in the number of graduates engaged in effective ministry. Of the graduates listed, 261 are noted to have enrolled in the theological department, and approximately 30 officially completed normal or theological course of study to be certified as graduates (Brawley, 1917, p. 149). Examining graduates between 1884 and 1915 as a composite of all prior graduates, there were 280 who were actively working, 90 of which were preaching and 75 employed as teachers. In other words, three-fifths of the graduates of the college were known to be engaged in Christian education, while another fifth were engaged in the work of the medical profession, YMCA work, or other lines of definite service (Brawley, 1917, p. 151).

In response to the social, political, and economic climates of 19th century United States in the West and South, Bishop Payne and President Robert developed an approach to higher education that reclaimed Christian views from those who used similar religious philosophies to exclude persons of color from participation in other social institutions. Bishop Payne used Christian education to create a moral and ethical environment to instill in his students a consciousness to guide their development into Christian adults fit for service in various fields. President Robert used Christian education as a means of motivating in his students a passion and desire for community service. They both used Christian ethics to train students to be productive citizens. Most importantly, Wilberforce University and Morehouse College produced graduates that would influence the future of race relations within the various Christian denominations in a larger struggle for equality and social justice. As leaders, these two presidents displayed the servant leadership traits of valuing people, developing people, building people, displaying authenticity, and sharing leadership.

The Support and Development of Students

Bishop Payne enjoyed a career noted for commitment to student success. His student-centered leadership approach began as a teaching style. He often reflected that his enthusiasm for education was the inspiration of his students (Payne, 1888, p. 23). He continued throughout his career to found schools creating opportunities for students to learn as he learned. Bishop Payne credited much of his early success to maintaining his own desire for new knowledge, and putting students' needs before his own (Payne, 1888, p. 25). While serving as president of Wilberforce University, Bishop Payne spent many days and nights considering the various challenges faced by his students. He believed that students needed every opportunity to express themselves as adults. He spent much of his time counseling, mentoring, and even teaching in the theology department. Regarding his interactions with students, Bishop Payne reflected upon his retirement: "But the most remarkable thing is the fact that all who have been trained in its halls and on its grounds from early childhood have proved themselves most thorough and accurate in scholarship; also most laborious, industrious, and thrifty" (Payne, 1888, p. 228).

Above all, Bishop Payne was proud of students' accomplishments, graduates, and nongraduates. He found pleasure in their newly found self-reliance and growing ambition that developed from the education they received at Wilberforce University. More important, Bishop Payne appreciated the Christian values instilled in each student and he treasured the contribution that Wilberforce University made to increase the numbers of theologically trained ministers in the AME church.

Assuming the leadership of a struggling seminary, President Robert was forced to rely on value in the students and their dedication to self-improvement. For the first 4 years of his presidency, President Robert led the institution without any assistance. He was the chief administrator, bookkeeper, groundkeeper, and principal teacher. Enrolling an average of 52 students annually over the same period, he heard the recitations of each student for 5 hours a day, and delivered two lectures a week on biblical and scientific subjects (Brawley, 1917, p. 25). The fact that he spent so much time working to develop students shows that he certainly had to have consistently sacrificed his own personal and familial needs.

President Robert labored intensely to improve the perception of the institution among the residents of the city of Augusta, the Baptist Church, and pastors in Black Baptist churches. His strategy was to ameliorate the perception by kindling in students the personal desire for a quality education. He inspired students to reach new levels of self-worth. This self-worth granted them confidence to use their gifts and knowledge in service to the local churches as teachers and preachers. Accordingly, the entire community valued the institution and President Robert's leadership. This motivation process was an important aspect as the seminary, during its early years, often enrolled the poorest and least academically prepared students in the South.

Bishop Payne and President Robert both worked to create curricular and co-curricular educational environments that inspired students to reach high levels of academic achievement. It is safe to observe from President Robert's use of various forms of intellectual stimulation, such as preaching invitations, and intense debates or external motivations, such as special guest lecturers and codes of conduct, display all six servant leadership traits.

Character Development and Staff Support

Bishop Payne prided himself in the development of his students. He believed that building character was just as important as intellect. Bishop Payne insisted that each student adhere to strict codes of conducts in order to build their character. Cited in the previous section, these rules focused on instilling in each student a reverence for Christian values and prepared them for the opportunities that a quality education would bring. Bishop Payne expected each student would be refined by their education and given a solid understanding of the social and cultural nuances of the period. Bishop Payne shares his reflections on the development of intellect and morality together:

> We have among us some very good people, and some very bad; some very intelligent, and some very ignorant; some who may be called stupid, and others who may be called learned. Let us now see what this generation is doing for the development of Christian education amongst us, and with it the development of Christian character. (Payne, 1891, p. 421)

It is on the basis of these lofty ideals, that Bishop Payne identified students as gentlemen and ladies. Heavily influenced by his travels across Europe and the United States, he believed that students must maintain a certain disposition to gain access to various opportunities. Students must, at all cost, avoid any behaviors that were associated with slavery. He vehemently opposed alcoholism, vagrancy, inappropriate contact with the opposite sex, loud talking, emotional worship and idleness, stigmas associated with slave culture. Hence, Wilberforce University established strict repercussions for inappropriate student behaviors (Wilberforce University, 1880–1, College Catalogue, p. 30). Certainly, Bishop Payne adhered to these standards by refraining from alcohol and other vices. However, his conservative nature was often seen as overly restrictive. In one instance, female students experienced more restrictions than male students, and often felt that they were ignored or discouraged from certain activities. This point is made in the historical sketch of the first Literary Society for Young Women:

> Wilberforce is one of the schools of our land which, in their capacity of Alma Mater (benign mother), do not, after heathen customs, seek to rear only sons, but extend the same care to the daughters. It is in all that relates to the education, the culture and the refinement of these daughters that we are especially interested.... The young men long ago organized the Sodalian, which lives, has increased and flourishes. There they have enjoyed literary advantages for years, gaining mental vigor and intellectual culture,

while their sisters have been standing still or only making such progress as they were able alone and unaided. (Payne, 1891, p. 443)

During his presidency, Bishop Payne acknowledged the success of male students and the contributions graduates made to the community and the church. However, no history is provided that references the impact of female students on the same community and church. Additionally, these standards also bore a heavy weight on the faculty. The annual teaching staff of Wilberforce between 1865 and 1876 was six, though the student population grew to approximately five hundred. Bishop Payne was skillful in recruiting skilled faculty and staff; however, due to low pay and lack of resources, Wilberforce University suffered much in the area of retention. The college history records gives proof:

> The changes amongst the instructors of Wilberforce University have been too many for its steady and uninterrupted progress and prosperity. Under the auspices of the AME Church, within twenty-two years, there have been in the presidency of Wilberforce three changes. In the office of lady principal and matron there have been nine changes. Among the instructors and professors there have been eleven changes. In the normal department there have been seven changes in the office of principal. (Payne, 1891, p. 446)

As outlined in the catalogue, most of the students' supervision was the responsibility of the faculty and a lady patron, who was responsible for daily management. However, with the constant turnover, Wilberforce University struggled to provide the necessary consistency to enforce Bishop Payne's Christian education model.

President Robert experienced many of the same successes and challenges as Bishop Payne. As cited throughout this chapter, the work of President Robert was held in high esteem by local church leaders and the Baptist church across the nation. He successfully proved that higher education was essential to rebuilding the Black community in the South. By 1879 the Atlanta Baptist Seminary attracted 245 men from across the country; however, lack of resources prevented the seminary from providing necessary boarding houses for students (Brawley, 1917, p. 27). As a result, students who choose to enroll in the college had to maintain their thrifty ways, often taking advantage of the kindness of the faculty and staff. With the Seminary's relocation to Atlanta in 1879, to what then was an industrial park, the supervision of students that was a hallmark of the institution was impossible. The relocation had various affects on the culture of the institution:

> The building moreover made no provision for dormitories. The students, even with the institution assisting, were forced to find boarding places where

they could, and, besides living in close and crowded houses, where the atmosphere was invariably far from intellectual and where sometimes they had to prepare their own meals, they were, except for the few hours of school each day, beyond the care of the teachers and generally exposed to the distractions and temptations of a rapidly growing city. (Brawley, 1917, p. 36)

President Robert witnessed a decrease in enrollment to 30 men by the Fall of 1880 and increase to 100 by the end of the year. The seminary also struggled with numerous changes in the faculty, as many left due to frustration at the low skill levels of students (Brawley, 1917, p. 41). Nevertheless, President Robert continued to use his resources to raise awareness and funds for the college, with the increasing support of the Black Baptist churches in Atlanta. By the time of President Robert's death in 1884, he was celebrated for producing over 500 Black educated and articulate male teachers, preachers, elected officials, and doctors across the United States and abroad.

Bishop Payne and President Robert faced various challenges to effectively train students; however, they experienced more triumph through the success of their graduates. To witness educational transformations, leaders must maintain patience, and learn to depict students' characteristics that are latent. Both leaders show evidence of displaying such patience and foresight. Therefore, the servant leadership traits of developing people and building people are evident in the achievement of Bishop Payne and President Robert.

Cultivating Meaningful Relationships

Founders of educational institutions must possess the ability to cultivate strong personal relationships. The above accounts provide proof that Bishop Payne and President Robert both excelled at this. They were diligent resourceful men who believed in the missions of their institutions and motivated others to participate in the work. Fundraising and community development provide a quality vantage point to observe the resourcefulness of these founding presidents. Bishop Payne on behalf of the AME church purchased Wilberforce from the ME church for $10,000.00, which was the total of its indebtedness. One schoolhouse was included in the purchase, though in good condition and suitable for the instruction of only approximately one hundred students. This central building included: recitation rooms, dormitories for teachers and students, culinary and bathing apartments, a laundry, and a chapel.

Despite the pleasant campus facility, Bishop Payne was immediately faced with the responsibility of raising funds to cover the purchase price and the cost of operation. Bishop Payne recalled:

When I made the bid for the property, I had not ten-dollar bill at my command, but I had faith in God. Within forty-eight hours after that act one hundred dollars was given us by Mrs. James Shorter, wife of Elder Shorter, and by June, 1863, we met the first payment of two thousand five hundred dollars. This sum was pledged and raised by the Baltimore and Ohio conferences. (Payne, 1888, p. 153)

Faith, as Bishop Payne called it, was a persistent reminder to the membership of the AME church that education was critical to the ultimate uplift of the race. Reminding each conference of this important mission the church faithfully supported with its finances, the purchase of Wilberforce, raising a total of $1,000.00 annually (Payne, 1891, p. 436). Unfortunately, on April 14, 1865 the building was burned and Bishop Payne was faced with the task of rebuilding an entire campus.

Over the next 13 years, Bishop Payne sought the assistance of men and women of every race, ethnic group, culture, religious tradition, and country. Primarily, he forged strategic relationships and partnerships to support the work of the university. His effort to cultivate relationships that benefited the university was five-pronged. First, Bishop Payne worked to bring as many dignitaries, elected officials, businessmen, and philanthropists to the campus as possible. He invited persons to be special lecturers, commencement speakers, and granted honorary degrees (Payne, 1888, p. 212). Second, Bishop Payne sought to develop the campus into a community of Black middle class who would re-invest in the campus by: providing services such as repairs and upkeep, rent property and offset other costs by free labor; and attract attention to Xenia, OH as an up and coming neighborhood for Black families to settle, from which the future student population would be recruited (Payne, 1888, p. 227). His community development work led Bishop Payne to acknowledge:

We are in the midst of a farming region, immediately encircled by ten families, who are educating their children in our school—some of them formerly students, who, since the left us, have married, and are now in their turn educating their children in their own Alma Mater. The influence of the College upon their children is manifest not only in their manners, but also in their talent. (Payne, 1891, p. 433)

Third, Bishop Payne traveled the United States and abroad speaking, publicly and privately, and publishing in every newspaper possible in an effort to spread the mission and accomplishments of the university. The essential message was that Wilberforce University was successful in empowering the Black community using education to build intellect and Christian character. As such, his audiences were dissuaded from ideas of colonization in Africa and emigration to the West Indies and Europe to support Reconstruction. Bishop Payne concluded that:

> At all places, whenever possible, it was my habit to speak upon the subject of domestic education—a subject which filled my mind and weighed heavily upon my heart, as it had from my early ministry, but never, perhaps, more so than since my experience as President of a college. (Payne, 1888, p. 213)

The fourth aspect is that Bishop Payne established the campus as a Christian mission field by starting an AME church on campus to raise funds through parishioner contributions and provide additional financial support to students and faculty (Payne, 1891, p. 436). Five, he sought government grants and gifts from the Freedmen's Bureau ($28,000.00) and other agencies such as, the Society for the Promotion of Collegiate and Theological Education ($1,800.00) and the American Unitarian Association ($4,000.00), who wanted to invest in legitimate Black community-based initiatives focused on self-empowerment (Payne, 1888, pp. 215, 228–229).

By 1876, through the efforts of Bishop Payne, Wilberforce University's assets included: 53 acres of real estate; ten buildings, exclusive of a barn and stable; a library with approximately 3,000 bound volumes; a museum in development; an endowment fund with approximately $25,000.00 in monetary gifts and stocks generated by the Wilberforce University Endowment Association. It was the first educational foundation to serve Black higher education to support two endowed professorships and bonds in the Western Union Telegraph Company and the railroad between Pittsburgh and Cleveland; and tuition fees and rents totaling $5,000.00 annually (Payne, 1891, p. 433).

> President Robert, after accepting the presidency of Atlanta Baptist Institute, had to use his mental and physical resources to build a college. The physical plant was in deplorable shape, no faculty were actively engaged, and student enrollment was down to five. President Robert reflected regarding the perception of the Institution in the following: The whole enterprise was looked upon with extreme disfavor by most of the white people in the community. By many, indeed, actual odium was associated with its assumed management. The buildings were dilapidated and in need of repair everywhere. There was not in them an article of furniture of any kind belonging to the institute. A few nails in the walls and a few books on a bench constituted the entire equipment. (Brawley, 1917, p. 23)

In other words, President Robert acknowledged that he had to build a college. The only good attached to the Institute at the outset of his presidency was the mission. As referenced in the previous chapter, he faced many challenges: the lack of administrative oversight and infrastructure; the lack of qualified faculty willing to teach in the South; constant treats by the KKK to harm the students, teachers, or physical structure; lack of support amongst the white Baptist churches for Black education; and, most important, the college had no funding to pay its debt, or provide for its needs (Brawley, 1917, p. 23). Rising to the task, President Robert developed a four-prong strategy to build a college.

First, President Robert worked to strengthen the relationship between the Institute and the ABHMS (Society). As stated in Chapter 4, the Institute was founded as part of the National Theological Institute, and was later fully merged as part of the educational mission work conducted by the Society. In its 1865 Annual Meeting, the Society voted and approved the following resolution:

> Resolved, That the Society will expect of its Executive Board that undeterred by any impracticable strict construction they should feel themselves bound to carry into effect in all wise and feasible ways the evangelization of the freedmen and to aid them in the erection or procurement of Church and school edifices when requisite. Resolved, That the Society will expect of all churches and associations connected with it a vigorous and hearty cooperation not only in raising the funds needed in the present exigency but also in commending to the Board for employment such fitting instruments—preachers, colporteurs and teachers—male and female as they know to be well qualified and faithful. (ABHMS, 1883, p. 404)

However, this support failed to manifest during the first half of President Robert's tenure. The resistance of Southern White Baptist preachers was based on their concern that the education of African-Americans implies the end of White social power.

Skillfully, President Robert worked to persuade this constituency group that the mission of the Institute is merely to complement their efforts and would in fact assist them in fulfilling their Christian duty. This position was a hard sell and his Baptist brothers in Georgia at once demurred and insisted that he looked to the North for money (Brawley, 1917, p. 24). Nevertheless, President Robert persisted and learned a valuable lesson which is to never accept no for an answer and to keep asking for support. He wrote over one hundred letters to Baptist ministers in the North and South, informing them of the good being done and the assistance needed. Eventually, financial aid came from various organizations and private donors. In essence, President Robert orchestrated, through his letter writing campaign, the college's first annual fund activity.

With consistent annual fundraising undertakings, President Robert was able to raise funds, amongst Whites and African Americans that provided for the repairs to the buildings, purchase of schoolroom and bedroom furniture, hiring of administrative staff and faculty, and payment of operational costs (Brawley, 1917, p. 24). These contributions and President Robert's political savvy eventually led to a book donation which contained 503 volumes; two $50 pledges, two $100 gifts; and, the establishment of scholarships by the New York State Colonization Society and other private donors (Brawley, 1917, pp. 26–27). Furthermore, President Robert was able to develop a strong relationship with the New York State Colonization Society that lasted throughout his tenure. The significance of this relationship cannot be overstated, for without the Society, the Institute could not have financially survived. The total support given to the college by the Society from 1869 to 1916 is totaled at $462,220.40, inclusive of: capital projects, special contribution by Negro friends, and grants made by the General Education Board of New York (Brawley, 1917, pp. 144–147).

Secondly, President Robert developed and encouraged support from the Black Baptist churches in Augusta. The Black Baptists of Georgia played an important role in the development of the college; however, prior to President Robert they made no financial contribution to the institution that is on record. President Robert's motto was that if the Black community would benefit most from the work of the Institute, then it should be obligated to support. Though this relationship began with small gifts, the giving of resources by members of the Black community remained consistent throughout the history of the college. The result for President Robert was an increased interest of Black Baptist ministers to participate in the administration of the college. In fact, by 1879, with the opening of the new school, the Southern Black Baptist influence on the college had grown so great that the Society reported that it was cooperating with the Missionary Baptist Convention of Georgia, the Black Baptist organization (Brawley, 1917, p. 33).

Third, President Robert worked to implement an administrative structure that is conducive to future support and growth. This was accomplished by reorganizing the Institute into a seminary in 1879. The major difference in the change of name is represented in the charter that states:

> The objects of the said corporation are to promote education among the colored people of the South, especially by the training of preachers and teachers of the colored race, and to this end, and to better accomplish its objects the corporation will establish and maintain such schools, colleges, and universities as it deems necessary. The corporation will transact its business in the City of Atlanta in said County of Fulton; it desires also the privi-

lege to have an office in the said City and County of New York; if it so wishes.
(Brawley, 1917, p. 161)

There are two points to infer from the above statement. The first point
is that the trustees seemed to have planned the establishment of other in-
stitutes: schools, colleges, and universities throughout the state to be associated with the newly formed seminary. The second one is that the trustees desired to maintain a presence in New York City, given that was the
headquarters of Rev. Dr. Morehouse, who was a trustee and secretary of
the Society. In either case the charter was accompanied by the board of
trustees' bylaws that outlined the election of a president and the framework
for governance. This feat was an important step for the college, as these
administrative actions created a sense among its supporters that it was seri-
ous about its mission, and had evolved into a mature educational institution
(Brawley, 1917, pp. 39–40).

The fourth strategy employed by President Robert attracted much
controversy. In 1879 the college established both its first official charter
and bylaws and relocated its campus from Augusta to Atlanta. The aim of
President Robert was to ensure that the college's growth is in tune with
the economic development activities and opportunities emerging in urban
America. Notwithstanding, the late 19th century saw market booms in busi-
ness associated with steel, lumber, and oil as a result of the industrial revolution across the United States. Atlanta was quickly developing as a city at
the center of textile import and export, especially as a railroad shifting yard
(Brawley, 1917, p. 35).

Many of the faculty and staff complained about the new site; however,
it was the vision of President Robert to be around such activity, as it was
necessary for increased visibility and access to resources. This was a shift
from the paradigm of college campuses centered in suburban areas to the
establishment of college campuses in the urban quarters. This shift allowed
students and faculty to enjoy the resources made available from city living.
The foresight in President Robert's approach was appreciated later when
the college was able to purchase fifteen additional acres in the area and
increase much of its student enrollment and faculty interest based on the
appeal of urban living.

Bishop Payne and President Robert's unmatched strategies to raise the
poor fiscal conditions of both institutions to the standard of American urban
universities provided opportunities to observe all servant leadership traits
in action. Bishop Payne and President Robert, in times of greatest challenges, showed evidence that they possessed the ability to not only develop
students, but also, to engage a community of stakeholders to participate

and contribute to their vision. Their efforts displayed the servant leadership traits of valuing people, developing people, building people, displaying authenticity, and sharing leadership.

Vision Setting and Implementation

Bishop Payne and President Robert have proven to possess Laub's (2000) servant leadership values by employing the above strategies to enhance the abilities of their respective colleges to effectively educate Black men and women. Dr. Laub reinforced the need of these values to have a corresponding effect on the institutions and the community as a whole. The focus of this section is to assess how servant leadership values create a culture for servant leadership to permeate the colleges. The theories of Dr. Greenleaf provide additional context for this analysis by considering how Dr. Greenleaf envisioned the adaptation of servant leadership to learning organizations. In the statement below, Greenleaf (1998) reflects on how his work incorporates servant leadership within universities and seminaries:

> If seminaries take on the full scope I will suggest, they will not at all be like universities. To be sure they have a curriculum of courses and they grant degrees. But this is incidental to their major function: to harbor and nurture prophetic voices that give vision and hope, and to serve as a sustaining support for churches. These are not primary functions of a university, and the university model may not be useful as a model for seminaries. (pp. 38–39)

Greenleaf's account is coherent with Laub's (2000) model—accentuating the importance of leadership values, displaying authenticity, providing leadership, and sharing leadership, together provides a framework to assess how an educational institution as a servant organization is meeting the standard, specifically to harbor and nurture prophetic voices.

Since Greenleaf (1998) does not provide a concrete definition for the term prophetic voice, it is more suitable to use one offered by Walter Brueggemann (2001) in the discipline of Religious Education. Brueggemann (2001) writes on the significance of a prophetic voice:

> In any case, my governing hypothesis is that the alternative prophetic community is concerned both with criticizing and energizing. On the one hand, it is to show that the dominant consciousness...will indeed end and that it is has no claim upon us. On the other hand, it is the task of the alternative prophetic community to present an alternative consciousness that can energize the community to fresh forms of faithfulness and vitality. (p. 59)

To develop prophetic voice in this context illustrates the ability of a servant leader to create a culture in the organization that both criticizes the dominant cultural consciousness, while invigorating the members of the organization to present an alternative way of thinking, acting and perceiving the same culture. In the case of Wilberforce University and Morehouse College, they have since their founding been considered educational institutions with a primary responsibility of providing Christian education. Furthermore, each Morehouse College and Wilberforce University remain connected to religious organizations, either via allocation of resources, or administrative oversight through trustee boards.

As such, Wilberforce University and Morehouse College have historically worked to perform Greenleaf's (1998) major function: harbor and nurture prophetic voices and support churches. Moreover, each Institution throughout its history, and at the time of their founding, has articulated a vision and community concern to combat unfavorable ways of thinking, acting, and perceiving towards the Black community. The AME church history articulates the prevailing outlook of the time concerning the importance of Wilberforce University in the following:

> This benevolent scheme is based on the supposition that the colored man must, for the most part, be the educator and elevator of this own race in this and other lands. Hence, a leading object of the institution is to educate and thoroughly train many of them for professional teachers, or for any other position or pursuit in life to which God, in his providences or by his spirit may call them. (Payne, 1891, p. 428)

Furthermore, the ABHMS at their Annual Meeting in 1865 voted and approved the following resolution:

> Resolved, That the Society will expect of its Executive Board that undeterred by any impracticable strict construction they should feel themselves bound to carry into effect in all wise and feasible ways the evangelization of the freedmen and to aid them in the erection or procurement of Church and school edifices when requisite. Resolved, That the Society will expect of all churches and associations connected with it a vigorous and hearty cooperation not only in raising the funds needed in the present exigency but also in commending to the Board for employment such fitting instruments— preachers, colporteurs and teachers—male and female as they know to be well qualified and faithful. (ABHMS, 1883, p. 404)

The primary purpose of the founders was to resist the institution of slavery, which was the dominant cultural consciousness of Reconstruction in the United States and their religious organizations. On the one hand the founding of the colleges were acts of protest by defying the dominant notion that slaves either could not, or should not be educated. On the other hand, the founding of these colleges were revolutionary acts, motivating the Black community to take an active responsibility in the future of their race post emancipation. Wilberforce University, founded by the all-Black AME church, and, Morehouse College, founded by the predominately White AB-HMS, provide two perspectives on the development of a prophetic voice on behalf of the Black community. Through the work of Bishop Payne and President Robert, each college was able to make distinct impacts on Black higher education in: (a) the preparation of religious leadership, (b) the shaping of Black identity, (c) the creation of a Black middle-class, and (d) the religious and educational training of women.

This section has been documenting the commitment of both Bishop Payne and President Robert to the preparation of religious leadership. Each leader believed in formal and Christian education. They both promulgated that the Black community had a right and responsibility to participate in the education of their religious leadership. They both advocated a curriculum that trained religious leaders in the liberal arts, sciences, and theology; and, they produced graduates who were committed to engaging in Christian service as teachers, preachers, doctors, lawyers, or any other chosen field to be agents of change in their local communities.

Certainly, the natural outcomes of such training and preparation were the new levels of self-perception acquired through quality education. Students were transformed, positively and negatively. As previously cited, both Wilberforce University and Morehouse College struggled with retention, as students gained enough knowledge to meet their immediate needs. Other students used their knowledge and new skills to chase fame and fortune, falling into various vices and negative behaviors. Yet, others, while completing their education training, experienced major personal transformation to become great leaders in society. The reflection of Rev. Morehouse on the work of the institution that is befitting of both colleges is noteworthy: "In my years of service I have seen the coarse boy become the talented preacher, the cultured professor, and the wise leader of thousands, and from long and wide acquaintance and observation I am prepared to say that the investment has paid a hundredfold." (Brawley, 1917, p. 159)

Accordingly, the mark of a Wilberforce University or Morehouse College graduate was a commitment to uplift the Black race. Indeed, graduates were expected to be exemplars of a quality Christian education; however, they too were expected to acquire a level of cultural refinement that would result in the creation of a Black middle class. As previously cited, both colleges went to great lengths to create a culture of excellence exemplified in disposition, dress, and deportment. Furthermore, each campus employed an administrator to oversee the development of proper social skills amongst students. Regulations and guidelines governing student life had a singular aim, namely to produce the best quality graduate possible. The artifacts of both colleges contain long lists of graduates and details of their work. Institutional pride centered on the success associated with one's graduates, and as such one's transformation from poor to middle class (Payne, 1891, pp. 430–431; Brawley, 1917, pp. 148–159).

However, during this time period, the attention given to the preparation of female leaders is often overlooked. In the case of Wilberforce University, it maintained its status as a co-educational institution. However, as previously cited, there were some distinct differences in the training of female students. Moreover, many of the aforementioned codes of conduct were targeted to prevent contact between the sexes. Students were discouraged from intermingling without a valid reason. It is noteworthy that Bishop Payne, while believing in the education of Black women, did not believe that Black women should be licensed to preach. No artifact is available to explain this contradiction, but his refusal to license a female preacher in the AME church, Rev. Jarena Lee, is recorded in her autobiography published in 1836, The Life and Religious Experience of Jarena Lee. Furthermore, the impact of his attitude toward female religious leaders was that as of 1891 no women were admitted into the theological department at Wilberforce University (Payne, 1891, p. 430). As previously cited, female students complained about not having a literary society, however, the reasons are due to the lack of sufficient numbers of interested students (Payne, 1891, p. 443).

In the case of Morehouse College, women were in attendance during its inception as the Augusta Baptist Institute, however, they were not officially counted as students (Brawley, 1917, p. 27). Upon President Robert's assumption of the presidency this practice ended, and the Institute was open to men only. As cited above, there are no artifacts to explain this decision; however, it is proof of the Southern Baptist position on the religious training of women for ministry. Despite this fact, there is evidence that the founders of the seminary, namely Rev. Frank Quarles, remained concerned about the preparation of female religious leaders. Accordingly, in a trustees' meeting on January 21, 1881, the members of the local board formally recommended to the ABHMS the founding of a seminary for women. The ABHMS, on March 10, 1881, voted and approved to authorize the Missionary Baptist Convention of Georgia to take the steps to raise $5,000.00 to build a school building for women on the grounds of the seminary (Brawley, 1917, pp. 47–48). The Atlanta Baptist Female Seminary officially began on April 11, 1881 and today is known as Spelman College.

This innovation allowed women to assume important roles at both colleges as administrators and teachers. Without the support of women like Mrs. James Shorter, Wilberforce University would not have received its first $100 gift (Payne, 1888, p. 153). Without the sacrifice of women like Miss Sherman, Miss Welch, and Miss Burt who traveled to Augusta, GA under threat by the KKK to be the first teachers of the Institute, Morehouse College would not have been able to open in 1867 (Brawley, 1917, p. 15). The legacy of these institutions is as much the legacy of Black women's continued support of the education of the Black community and the heritage of the men whose perspective dominates the historical accounts.

Conclusion

Colleges and universities in general are social organisms, and are therefore the products of their cultural environments. They are created to service the educational needs of specific populations. Colleges and universities are unique in their mission, purpose, vision, commitment, and most important, their leadership. Defined as such, Black colleges founded during Reconstruction in the United States, fit Laub's (2000) definition of a servant organization.

Leadership of any higher educational institution requires: (a) a willingness to cope with a unique set of challenges, transforming them into organizational success; (b) an openness of all stakeholders to personal and institutional transformation; (c) a willingness of all stakeholders to evolve and expand their knowledge to incorporate fresh understanding of their community and environment; and (d) a leadership team that maintains a conviction to lead change despite the opposition, or obstacles that may arise. These criteria fulfill the servant leadership profile used in the Organizational Leadership Assessment (OLA) model to facilitate analysis. Furthermore, Bishop Payne and President Robert successfully used their servant leadership values to produce institutions that continue to impact Black education.

6

Implications and Meanings for Higher Education

This chapter sets out to answer the research question: "What can we learn from the impact of Wilberforce University and Morehouse College on Black higher education over the last 150 years?" In order to answer this question, this segment of the project will reflect on lessons learned from the founding of Wilberforce University and Morehouse College in order to make some recommendations for future research in Black higher education in the United States.

Summary of Findings

The Evolution of Black Education

The emergence of Black education during Reconstruction was the outgrowth of a pre-existing struggle for Black self-improvement and community empowerment. On the basis of primary sources such as letters, journals, newspapers, and autobiographies, it is reasonable to infer that freedmen

Not For Ourselves Alone, pages 115–126
Copyright © 2019 by Information Age Publishing
All rights of reproduction in any form reserved.

perceived education as a vehicle to acquire freedom. Given that slaves had no civil right to an education, the earliest forms of Black education were thus: secret literacy societies and one-on-one tutorials, plantation management, workforce development, agricultural and technical skill building, and religious education.

Black education shaped the cultural experience and expectations of freedmen and served as a means to provide African Americans the intellectual means to access: (a) social privilege, (b) forms of protest, (c) civil rights, and (d) reparation. The acquisition of these privileges was conducive to a new sociocultural reality within the Black community. This cultural progress is obvious in the historical mini-narratives offered in Chapter 3. From slavery to emancipation, Reconstruction to segregation, and desegregation to civil rights, the mini-narratives connect the successive periods that shaped the evolution of Black higher education into the sociocultural legacy of Black people. The influence of Black education on Black culture may be assessed through the types of educational opportunities given to slaves, types of social relationships between master and slave classes, slave insurrection, escapism and cultural assimilation, impact of education on slaves, and the effect of Black education on the deterioration of the plantation system.

Emerging from the institution of slavery, emancipation provided a renewed hope for unrestricted and government supported Black empowerment. As such, the most important legacy of Reconstruction history in the United States was the birth of formal Black education. This is evident in the stories of slaves, either being educated by their liberal masters, or escapees who were self taught; education for Black people in the 19th century was a coveted commodity. The majority of African Americans believed education would not just improve, but transform their lives.

The historical accounts and evidences of the previous chapters prove that the continued debate over the role of Black labor in post-emancipation society, specifically, in the South and the question—"How can freedmen be effectively integrated into a market economy that allows them to prosper directly from their own labor?"—were at the heart of Reconstruction history. The attempts to answer this question were articulated in a series of constitutional, legal, political, and social clashes between Blacks and Whites, Northerners and Southerners, Union loyalists and Confederate patriots, industrialists, and plantation owners. The entire country was divided over the profits of Black labor. This project focused on assessing the impact of Black higher education on the Black freedom movement as they both developed during Reconstruction.

This project has argued, in Chapters 3 and 4, the following historical developments. Emancipation (Black freedom) led to the creation of Black labor. The creation of Black labor established a working class seeking more social and political influence, and independence. Once self-employed, empowered freedmen set out to control their own fates and participate as full citizens in the United States, which gave rise to Black suffrage. The fact that African Americans were refused the right to vote while participating in the society built by their free labor caused Black suffrage movements to become more radicalized and gave rise to ideologies of Black power. Black power evolved into Black empowerment—the creation of Black-owned businesses, founding of churches, and communities organized to facilitate self-help and community improvement. Black organizations cultivated Black pride, the founding of Black educational institutions to preserve their cultural scripts and provide mechanisms to further Black liberation and the development of Black consciousness. Black people, with the assistance of Northern Whites, used education to achieve political involvement, social integration, economic improvement, leadership development, and espouse the social values and norms of Black culture.

Bishop Payne, President Robert, and Black Higher Education

Black education was built on the foundation of freedmen' self-reliance and deep-seated desire to create, control, and sustain schools for themselves and their children. As such, the history of Black higher education in the United States cannot be considered apart from the men and women who wrote it with their lives. The main focus of this historical research project is to chronicle the lives of two such men, Bishop Payne and President Robert. This project sought to tell the stories of their personal and professional development, compare and contrast their experiences, and assess the impacts of their legacies on the specific institutions they served and Black higher education in general.

The historical artifacts on these two men and institutions provided valuable insight into their commitment to Black education, Christian education, and the development of Black leaders. As individuals, their motivations to pursue careers in education started during their adolescence and continued until their death. Bishop Payne and President Robert were committed to carry out cultural change and to leave a legacy for future generations.

The task of each president was different. Their institutions were in different regions, maintained slightly different missions, operated under different organizational and reporting structures. Also, their institutions were influenced by different local and state politics and maintained different cohorts of student enrollment. Though, these institutions were similar in that they both competed for limited resources, struggled to create curriculums that met their students' needs and skill levels, maintain connection to religious bodies while remaining committed to Black higher education.

Impacts, Implications, and Recommendations

The leadership experiences of Bishop Payne and President Robert teach us some significant lessons. Moreover, since Wilberforce University and Morehouse College are still in operation, it is thus possible to assess the impacts of the founding leadership on the 150-year legacies of their respective institutions. Bishop Payne and Rev. Dr. Robert have mostly shaped the legacy of their respective institutions in three areas; namely, (a) organizational leadership, (b) mission integrity, and (c) creating an enduring legacy.

Organizational Leadership

Theories of education and community leadership center on the following key concepts: maintenance of stability and order in the social system, use of biological organisms as metaphors, the necessity of society's adaptive abilities to ensure survival and evolution through states of equilibrium, social systems which use shared norms and values to legitimate human participation, social systems which institutionalize behaviors through social functions, and culture as an integrated body of knowledge, pseudo-knowledge, beliefs and values through which human life is lived (Coppola, 2005, p. 32). Under the light of these key concepts, Bishop Payne and President Robert, through their institutions, provide two models for how servant leadership can be effectively applied to the scientific management of Black higher educational institutions.

It is undeniable that no individual or institution could escape being affected by the various changes occurring during Reconstruction. Although this time was traumatizing for African Americans yet, they hoped that certain individuals and institutions could articulate visions and missions that are conducive to the empowerment of the Black community. Furthermore, in light of Du Bois' (1938) challenge to Black higher education, administrators realized by the late 19th to mid-20th century that social progress was not predicated upon change among the workers and followers alone; rather, raising academic quality depended upon critical reflection on the leadership and mission of colleges and universities in the United States. The use of scientific management by university administrators resulted in the practice of leadership being considered a determinant factor of institutional effectiveness. The aim of successful organizations' sustained management was to achieve innovative strategies that are conducive to cultural change.

Despite the state of affairs at both Wilberforce University and Morehouse College during their inception Bishop Payne (1863) and President Robert (1871) embarked on ambitious plans to create institutions to innovate the social experiences of Black people. Through Black higher education, they both intended to promote the intellectual equality of Black people to those of other races. They both adopted a servant leadership model that sought to (a) develop strategic partnerships with their founding religious organizations to raise funds for capital projects and the support of the most intellectually advanced students; (b) partner with the surrounding Black religious and civic organizations and connect the institutions to the community; (c) create an organizational structure to sustain growth, ensure increased enrollment, and support of institutional needs; and (d) emphasize the importance of developing practical experience, creating local mission fields through civic engagement opportunities, internships, and work opportunities for students.

The import of these two institutions, which were founded during the mid-19th century, ought to be the basis of future research comparing various types of Black higher educational institutions. The 19th and 20th century produced a rich and diverse tradition of colleges and universities. The study of Black higher education would greatly benefit from a comparison of the infrastructure and operations of modern-day colleges with colleges which were founded during the 19th century. It is imperative to compare and contrast the servant leadership styles of these founders with those found in leadership of the era to acquire the best suitable model for Black higher educational institutions. It is not in the purview of this study to consider presidents who served after the founders, however, research on succeeding leadership would add to the history of the colleges studied and provide data on the importance of the consistency of institutional's vision and mission.

An example of a potential research study would be a comparison of Wilberforce University and Morehouse College from 1885 to 1905. This study would evaluate the leadership of these institutions at the turn of the century, assessing how subsequent presidents maintained the founding presidents' mission, vision, and servant leadership values. Another study of interest would compare and contrast Atlanta University, Howard University, Hampton University, Lincoln University, and Tuskegee University. These Black higher educational institutions are suitable for study because they were each founded during Reconstruction and maintained distinct missions and their founding presidents were successful in shaping institutional legacies worthy of consideration.

Mission Integrity and the Big Black Investment

Since the late 18th century, historians have noted tensions in theories of Black higher education over the issue of how best to invest in Black children. Investing in education included two concerns: (a) increasing social capital and (b) using their prophetic voice to ensure the future viability of Black people. Liberal arts and religious education institutions founded between 1850 and 1870 and the shift to agricultural and industrial focused institutions founded between 1870 and 1910 illustrate how Black higher education was often viewed as the means to transform the Southern economy from a dependence on slave labor to a more skilled workforce (Bullock, 1970, p. 165).

Bishop Payne and President Robert showed great concern for increased investment in Black education through their leadership. Schultz (1961) identifies skill, knowledge, and similar attributes as quality components that affect human capabilities to be productive. Investing resources in these components enhance their effectiveness, while increasing the value and productivity of labor to yield a positive rate of return (p. 8). Furthermore, historians of freedmen's education argued that a major motivation for Northern activism was economic. The White leaders of aid societies and religious denominations were often businessmen and manufactures. They assumed that educated men and women had greater material appetites and would buy Northern products to satiate them. This assumption was the basis of investments in Southern Black education as a means to open new markets; incorporating the Black community in the consumer market was considered as the most important reason for the education of Negroes (Butchart, 1980, p. 56).

Wilberforce University and Morehouse College were similar in crafting missions to focus on granting the Black community the required skills, tools, and competencies to be productive citizens and change agents. Emphasis on training Black men and women who could improve the Black community were central to these respective missions.

However, Bishop Payne and President Robert were wise not to establish their respective college's after the traditional European model; instead, they created servant leader organizations. As servant leader institutions, the missions of Wilberforce University and Morehouse College included a commitment to addressing cultural and social inequalities. In essence, they were founded to be a prophetic voice in setting out to raise Black consciousness through a continued fight for Black liberation and economic empowerment.

Within this paradigm, Black education stands as a social responsibility and often equated with race consciousness. The major concern of this paradigm is the character of Black educational institutions, more specifically: Is their purpose the liberation and betterment of the Black race? Or the production of a new working class? Every Black college or university founded post-Reconstruction had to grapple with this concern. In the case of Wilberforce University and Morehouse College, both missions focused on the creation of Black leaders. Each institution purposefully used Black higher education to create a new Black elite, rather than a new working class. This purpose generates significant debates within the Black community.

One author who took up this debate is E. Franklin Frazier (1929, 1942, and 1948) in his work on the Negro College and the Black Bourgeoisie deemed the efforts of Black colleges to increase Black social capital problematic. Frazier (1938) argued that the emergent Black middle class and businessmen sought to take advantage of segregation by exploiting Black workers without White competition (p. 497).

Frazier's accurate yet incomplete description tarnished the perception of the Black middle class, whose existence is a direct result of the Black college. The majority of the Black bourgeoisie were graduates of Black colleges, and as such, provided the community with examples of success apart from White dominated society (Smith & Bender, 2008, p. 126).

The direct benefits of this study are the various unexpected findings related to the founding presidents' attempts to improve the social status of freed people. Bishop Payne and President Robert found creative strategies to resolve issues related to fundraising, faculty recruitment and retention, student enrollment, engagement and persistence, physical plant, academic quality, and service learning. These are unique in that they proved, on the one hand, that Black students could achieve academic success without similar access to resources as their White counterparts. On the other hand, strategies employed by these presidents proved that Black colleges were the best solution for improving the social, political, and economic conditions of the Black community.

The strategies above remain issues in American higher education. Additional research on Black college and university presidents would provide valuable insight into how practitioners have forged successful paradigms of Black student success. In fact, since the 1970s an increasing number of

Black students have opted to attend majority White colleges. Subsequently, critics of Black higher education have questioned the need for Black colleges, particularly institutions that have performed poorly on accreditation and student success evaluations. Administrators at Black colleges with high student performance cited students' increase in confidence as a significant and distinguishing factor of Black higher education (Smart, 2004, p. 21). Since, this confidence is interchangeable with Black pride, it is difficult to measure. One alternative is to study the methods and practices employed by various presidents to instill, foster, and/or cultivate confidence in students.

Leadership, Academic Excellence, and Christian Education

As mentioned throughout this study, the mission of Black higher education during Reconstruction was the training and preparation of leaders. These leaders provided the necessary intellectual capital to understand and respond to the critical issues facing the Black community, while maintaining Christian values and morals.

Bishop Payne's commitment to Black empowerment is evident in the many articles, papers, sermons, and speeches he published. He was an influential leader, not only of Wilberforce University and the AME church, but the Black freedom movement as well. He was an exemplar of the Black intellectuals' responsibility to understand and respond to critical issues facing people of color in the United States and abroad. Bishop Payne grasped that the general mission of the university was Black community empowerment based on the supposition that people of color must be the primary initiators and educators of their own race in this country and beyond (Payne, 1969, p. 428). Furthermore, the AME church in its efforts to promote Christian education asked each of its Conferences to form education committees to advance the cause by the creation of Sunday schools, secondary schools, and colleges.

The vision of Morehouse College, under the leadership of President Robert, can be summarized in one statement: He sought to develop the Augusta Institute into a well- respected 4-year liberal arts college in the United States that grants Black men the skills, tools, and competencies to be successful ministers and teachers. Essentially, Black higher educational institutions must create leaders, and even more specifically servant leaders who understand the importance of Black education and how to train young people to assume leadership positions. Bishop Payne and President Robert both shared this concern, incorporating it in the mission, management, and culture of their respective institutions. Moreover, they both developed and maintained a commitment to Christian higher education and the moral and ethical preparation of leaders.

This study focused on two religious organizations and their roles in supporting the founding of these institutions. Future research should consider other religious organizations, and denominations that founded Black higher educational institutions during and after Reconstruction, to assess how they developed approaches to Christian education. An example of research on this subject would be a study on Virginia Union of the United Methodist Church, Xavier University of the Catholic church, Edward Waters College of the AME church and other historically Black colleges founded by religious denominations. Moreover, the study of Black higher education would benefit from research on the impacts of church polity, race, theology, ideology, and geography on the founding of these institutions.

This type of study would examine the above impacts and provide analysis of the colleges' contributions to the community, Black higher education, and Black religious experience. The findings would provide each of these colleges an opportunity to reflect on their mission, identifying aspects of their institutional religious identity that may have eroded over the years. Institutions may also use these findings to strengthen student and alumni engagement, reclaiming their religious legacy, and historical uniqueness. This research would be useful to the field of Black higher education, as it will result in professional dialogue and new scholarship on the benefits and challenges of moral, ethical, and religious education on today's college campuses. Ultimately, research on this topic would provide a platform to discuss how denominational affiliations impact Black colleges.

Creating a Living Legacy

Creating a quality higher educational institution that fulfills its promise of student success is as much about ensuring the effectiveness and efficiency of the management process, given that it is about assessing the quality of outcomes. In the case of Black higher education, the process of creating leaders is reflected in the curriculum and success is measured by the quality of graduates. Bishop Payne and President Robert showed great concern for ensuring that graduates pursue successful careers and embody the best of the Black community.

As part of their curricular experience, students at Wilberforce University and Morehouse College took an active part in Sunday schools of their city and other states. Bishop Payne and President Robert are considered pioneers of the service learning movement in higher education by encouraging civic engagement. Each student received significant training from internship experiences. Bishop Payne is noted for creating a church on campus for students to hone their craft under the faculty's mentorship. President Robert is noted for his use of service learning to develop a reputation of his graduates for being quality orators and theologians. This resulted in Morehouse College's students being in high demand to preach and teach at local churches.

Overall, the mark of a Wilberforce University or Morehouse College's graduate was a commitment to the uplift of the Black race. Indeed, graduates were expected to be exemplars of a quality Christian education and members of the emerging Black middle-class. While this study focused on two founding presidents, it did not consider other presidents who founded, or assumed their leadership roles at Black higher educational institutions during the same time period, 1863 to 1884. The field of higher education administration would greatly benefit from a study on other presidents and colleges founded during Reconstruction. The ideal goal of such a study would be to compare and contrast findings to assess the total impact of Black higher education on the social context of the time period.

Furthermore, the field of educational leadership lacks research on the personal and professional lives of the men and women who have led Black colleges and universities. With the myriad of critical issues facing Black higher education today, future historical research projects detailing the experiences of Black college presidents would be of tremendous benefit. Robert Franklin (2007), president of Morehouse College in Atlanta, GA in his book *Crisis in the Village* points to significant challenges currently facing HBCUs. For him, these challenges are the following: decline in enrollment generally; decline in the number of African-American students enrolled specifically; increase in leadership turnover (position advertisements and vacancies); discontent between administration and faculty over work environment; lack of mission identification, authenticity, and integration; reduced access to private funding sources; and the lack of quality in the academic enterprise (p. 184). A study of this sort would be useful in assessing how President Franklin and his colleagues have developed the best practices for educational leadership, higher education administration, and Black higher education.

Conclusion

Not for Ourselves Alone

The cultural legacy of the African-American community is embodied in their educational entrepreneurship. Post emancipation and throughout

Reconstruction to the close of the 19th century, African Americans developed institutions and organizations to support communal and self-empowerment. As one of these institutions, Black higher educational institutions were created to provide training and preparation for personal, social, political, cultural, and economic improvement. This point of educational entrepreneurship is amplified by Cynthia Jackson and Eleanor F. Nunn (2003) who observe that of the 103 HBCUs currently operating, approximately 75% were established between 1865 and 1899 and over 90% are located in the South, arising in response to the reality of Black exclusion from White institutions in the North and South (p. 3).

Throughout the approximate four hundred-year history of enslavement, racial discrimination, and social injustice, African Americans have managed to develop a pioneering, innovative, and resourceful spirit that resulted in numerous remarkable contributions to American society. Furthermore, the election of the first African-American president of the United States, in the 21st century, imbues this history with greater significance and transforms it into a social success script which is useful for other cultural minorities.

This historical research project provided an account of two pioneering leaders and institutions of Black higher education. The findings and lessons learned are testimonies of their commitments to leave a legacy for following generations. These leaders had deep religious beliefs and convictions; they understood their life's work was not for themselves alone, rather, that the outcome would benefit their people, nation, and the global community. This project concludes with some key words from the men whose lives have made this study possible—Bishop Payne and President Robert. Bishop Payne reflected on his work at Wilberforce University and in the AME church:

> But what will be the use of these recollections of men and things; what of these reflections on them if they will not awaken some slumbering boy; if they fail to excite the latent faculties of a sportive lad; if they be not effective in stimulating the energies of some youth, who having strong, pure, good blood flowing from a large, broad heart through his entire body, is by nature fitted to accomplish good things for man and earth? (Payne, 1881, p. 335)

Brawley (1917) credits his knowledge of the history of Morehouse College's founding years to a pamphlet written by President Robert, *Historical Sketch of the Augusta Institute* (p. 160). Even though, no direct quote from President Robert is available, we do have the words of the trustees who, after his death, issued a formal resolution stating:

When the subject of assuming the delicate and responsible position of the presidency of what is now known as the Atlanta Baptist Seminary was presented to him, it was considered in the light of duty, and in accepting it he brought into his work, with the experience and culture of a lifetime, all the enthusiasm of an ardent nature sanctified by divine grace. To the wisdom, tact, and energy displayed by him in the management of the Seminary is due, under the favor of God, the prosperous condition in which he left it and the present hopeful outlook for its future usefulness. (Brawley, 1917, p. 38)

APPENDIX

Wilberforce University Historical Artifacts

Board of Trustees Minutes, 1865–1886

Not For Ourselves Alone, pages 127–143
Copyright © 2019 by Information Age Publishing
All rights of reproduction in any form reserved.

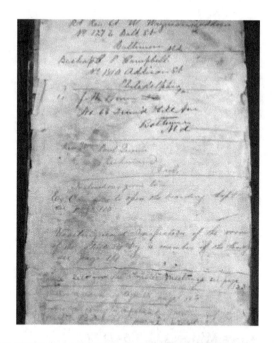

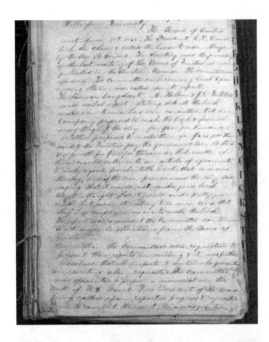

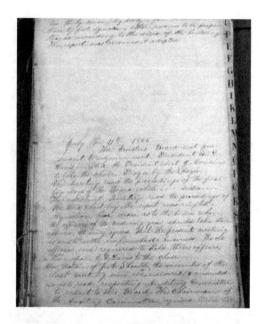

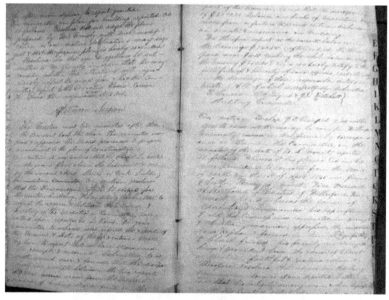

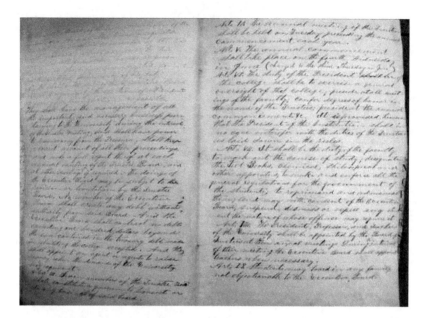

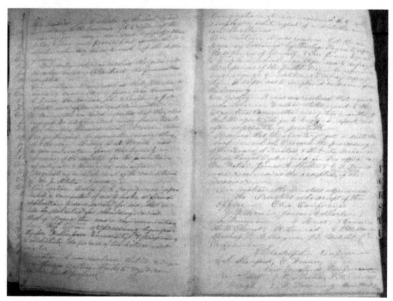

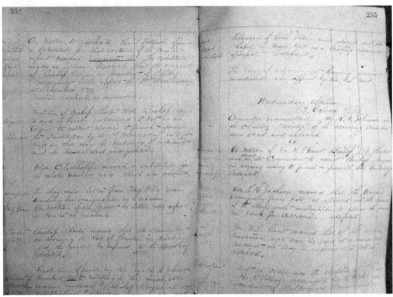

On motion to adopted, Rev P. Tolliver offered a substitute for that section of the Com[mittee] report marked Suggestion 20. The substitute reads as follows. Resolved, That the resignation of Bishop Payne as President of Wilberforce University take effect the 1st Wednesday in September 1876.
Motion adopted as amended.

Motion of Bishop Shorter that Bishop Payne be and is hereby impowered to act as an Agent to collect monies to finish & furnish the Institution by the 1st Wednesday in Sept and on that day the building to be dedicated

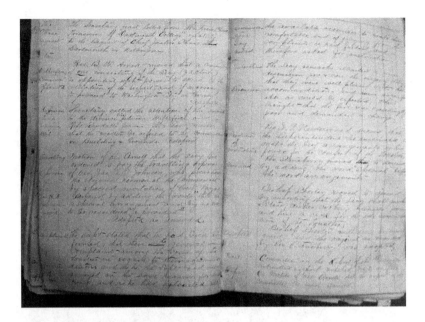

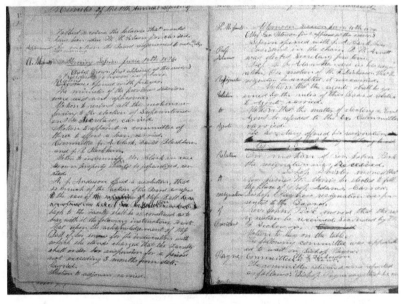

College Catalogue, 1881

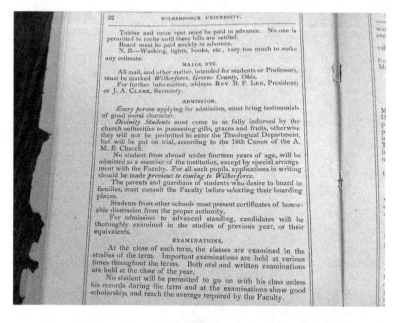

32   WILBERFORCE UNIVERSITY.

Tuition and room rent must be paid in advance. No one is permitted to recite until these bills are settled.

Board must be paid weekly in advance.

N. B.—Washing, lights, books, etc., vary too much to make any estimate.

MAILS, ETC.

All mail, and other matter, intended for students or Professors, must be marked *Wilberforce, Greene County, Ohio.*

For further information, address Rev. B. F. Lee, President; or J. A. Clark, Secretary.

ADMISSION.

Every person applying for admission, must bring testimonials of good moral character.

Divinity Students must come to us fully indorsed by the church authorities as possessing gifts, graces and fruits, otherwise they will not be permitted to enter the Theological Department, but will be put on trial, according to the 10th Canon of the A. M. E. Church.

No student from abroad under fourteen years of age, will be admitted as a member of the institution, except by special arrangement with the Faculty. For all such pupils, applications in writing should be made *previous to coming to Wilberforce.*

The parents and guardians of students who desire to board in families, must consult the Faculty before selecting their boarding places.

Students from other schools must present certificates of honorable dismission from the proper authority.

For admission to advanced standing, candidates will be thoroughly examined in the studies of previous year, or their equivalents.

EXAMINATIONS.

At the close of each term, the classes are examined in the studies of the term. Important examinations are held at various times throughout the terms. Both oral and written examinations are held at the close of the year.

No student will be permitted to go on with his class unless his records during the term and at the examinations show good scholarship, and reach the average required by the Faculty.

EXPENSES.

Tuition in Practice School	$3 00
Tuition in Sub-Academic Department	4 75
Tuition in Academic, Normal and Scientific	5 75
Tuition in Classical	6 75
Room Rent, per Term of 14 Weeks	2 25
Washing, per Dozen	75
Incidentals, per Term	25
Wood, per Cord	$3 to $4

Coal, 15c. to 18c. per Bushel—Coal-bin, 75c. per Year.

BOARD.

Board can be obtained for $1.50 or $2.00 per week. There is connected with the school, a boarding hall which is run in the interest of the students, *i. e.*, that they may procure cheap, yet good and substantial board. To those who go on duty, board $1.50 per week, otherwise $2.00. To keep the boarding hall in good condition each student is charged an initiation fee of $1.50; in other words, the first week's board is $3.00, with no extra charges thereafter. Several of the teachers board in the hall, one of them managing it. It is our object to make this hall not only a means of economy, but an effectual source of culture.

SUMMARY.

Tuition, per School Year	$ 9 00	$20 25
Room Rent, per School Year	6 75	6 75
Board, per School Year	61 50	81 50
Fuel, per School Year	8 00	12 00
Total		

Great care is taken to guard the pupils from immoral habits, profane language, and reading improper books.

The religious element will receive particular encouragement and protection. No repulsive sectarianism will be indulged. While such a disposition will be discountenanced, there will be assiduous efforts to favor and render inviolate the profession of Christianity, and to induce those who are not truly religious to become so. To all inclined to respect the Christian religion and its institutions, the welcome hand will be heartily extended; but to those whose influence is prejudicial to religion and good morals, no protracted stay can be allowed; believing, as we do, that the success of an educational enterprise is strictly proportional to its moral and religious tone.

FURNITURE, ETC.

Each room is furnished with a clothespress, bedstead, mattress, two pillows, stove, table and two chairs.

Young ladies are advised to provide themselves with overshoes and waterproof cloaks. Students should bring their own bed-clothing, towels, etc., with names marked in full.

GENERAL INFORMATION.

LOCATION.

Wilberforce is three and a half miles northeast of Xenia, which is on the Little Miami R. R., sixty-five miles from Cincinnati, and fifty five miles from Columbus, hence it has direct communications with all parts of the United States The Mineral Springs, and other natural surroundings, afford at the same time both a most beautiful and healthful location.

RELIGIOUS INSTRUCTION.

At 7:45 A. M., and 4 P. M., all the pupils assemble in the chapel for religious devotion, which consists in reading a portion of the Scriptures, singing a hymn, and prayer; at which all are required to be present. These exercises have a most happy influence upon the pupils, and have done much in making the labors of governing comparatively light.

30

PROHIBITIONS.

1. The association with the opposite sex without permission.
2. The use of intoxicating drinks, tobacco, fire-arms, or other deadly weapons; games of chance, profanity and obscenity.
3. The use or possession of any immoral books or papers.
4. Visiting each other's rooms during study hours.
5. Absence from premises, or visiting families without permission.
6. All improper conduct.
7. Cutting, marking, or in any way defacing the building or its appurtenances.
8. Visiting the kitchen without permission.
9. Throwing water, trash, litter, or anything offensive from the window.

All unexcused delinquencies are registered, and when the number amounts to *five*, or *any number more than five*, and less than *ten*, notice thereof is to be given to the student and to his parent or guardian. When the number of unexcused delinquencies amounts to *ten* the student ceases to be a member of the University. Any student who marries while pursuing studies at the University, ceases to be a member of the same.

REQUIREMENTS.

1. Proper observance of the Sabbath—attendance at Church and Sabbath School.
2. Bathing and all preparations for the Sabbath must be faithfully attended to on Saturday evening.
3. Punctual attendance at prayers, recitations and other exercises.
4. Strict observance of the appointed study hours.
5. Every student will be held responsible for all improper conduct occuring in his room, and particularly accountable for all injury beyond ordinary use.
6. Every room must be accessible at all times to the members of the Faculty.
7. Students must keep their rooms and the dormitory halls in good order, and leave them clean at end of term. All must assits in keeping the halls and school-room clean and comfortable.
8. Students must rise in the morning at the ringing of the first bell, cleanse and set their rooms in order for the day, before study hours commence.

✕ *The government is inflexibly strict in excluding all practices tending to immorality, and in exacting a uniform regard for good order, studious habits, and attention to the prescribed routine of duty.* ✕ Every student, but particularly such as are of immature years, receives the individual and prayerful watch-care of members of the Faculty. Wholesome regulations are instituted, designed to promote the prosperity and happiness of the students; which will commend themselves to every well-disposed mind, and receive the cordial support of every *lady and gentleman.* A disposition to *evade* just and salutary rules will meet with special disapprobation.

In the work of instruction, as well as of discipline, our aim is to inspire and increase in the pupils self-respect, self-control and self-developement.

A daily account is kept of each student in such a way as to afford a full exhibit of his habits in regard to regularity and punctuality, as well as the merit and demerit of his relations each day, in his several studies. A monthly report will be sent to the parents, or guardian of each pupil.

REQUIREMENTS.

1. Proper observance of the Sabbath—attendance at Church and Sabbath School.

2. Bathing and all preparations for the Sabbath must be

Ethics (completed)..Green
Hebrew—Grammar and Chrestomathy...
Hermeneutics...
Symbolics and Church Polity...
[Biblical Exercises given throughout the Junior and Senior years.]

The French is made one of the regular studies of the Theological Classes, in order that they may be excited to consider and labor for the Protestantism of Hayti, so as to wrest that gem of the ocean from the grasp of Roman Catholicism, and the semi-heathenism which now degrades the uneducated massess of its population.

We believe that the scientific character of this course will give our Theological graduates a greater ability to meet and vanquish modern infidelity No one can enter into conflict with the infide

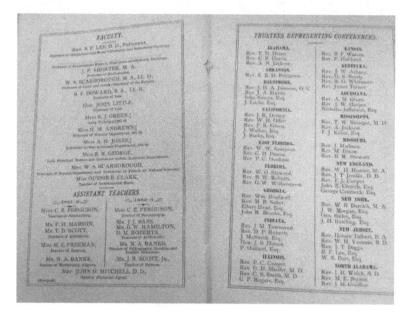